AF574379

VIPER

A JESSICA JAMES MYSTERY

KELLY OLIVER

VIPER

A Jessica James Mystery

By Kelly Oliver

Copyright © 2020, Kelly Oliver

All rights reserved.

Published by KAOS PRESS at kaospress.com

No parts of this publication may be reproduced, stored in a retrieval system, or transmitted in any form or by any means, electronic, mechanical, photocopying, recording, or otherwise, without the prior written permission of the copyright owner.

This is a work of fiction. Any similarity between the characters and situations within its pages and places or persons, living or dead, is unintentional and co-incidental.

Print ISBN number: **978-0-9975836-8-7**

Ebook ISBN number: **978-0-9975836-6-3**

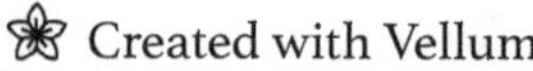
Created with Vellum

JESSICA JAMES MYSTERIES (BOOK 5)

Be careful, lest in casting out your demon you exorcise the best part of you.

—Friedrich Nietzsche

1

The flashing cursor on the blank computer screen was like an accusing finger wagging at her. *Come on, Jessica, do it. Write something. Anything.* She sat gnawing on the cap of her ballpoint pen. Thinking about the meaning of life made her want to bite down hard on something, like a movie cowboy getting a bullet removed without anesthesia. Usually, she went for her fingernails, but she'd sworn off biting her nails last summer when a jagged edge caught on Mayhem's halter and nearly ripped her fingernail clean off. If only she had as much willpower when it came to her dissertation. Jessica's hands hovered over the keyboard as she hoped for inspiration. As usual, she had second thoughts. With so many people hurt and hungry, who cared about philosophy? What good did this scholarly crap do anyone?

Maybe her mom was right and she should move

back home and get a "real job." Thinking of her mom stuck in the crummy Alpine Vista trailer park on the backside of nowhere strengthened her resolve. She was going to write this damn dissertation, get her degree, and get a teaching job far away from the boonies of Montana. She tapped her computer awake. At this rate, it could take another decade to finish her dissertation . . . she'd be in her thirties by then. An old lady. She only had one more chapter to write. *Why is it so hard to finish this damned thing?*

Jessica couldn't take the intimidating blank screen and the cursor's shaming flash for another minute, so she shifted her gazed to the colorful bakery case, where vegetable-laden muffins and cakes tempted her to take a break from writing . . . or not writing. One advantage of writing (or not writing) in the café was there was always food and drink, unlike her efficiency apartment, with its pint-size refrigerator filled with moldy cheese and taking up half her closet. And the air-conditioning worked at the café, which wasn't always true for her apartment. The hottest September on record, and her third-floor walk-up was like a toaster oven. Here, the cool breeze coming from the vent overhead helped keep her awake, despite German philosophy's best attempts to lull her to sleep.

She thought of Jack, rotting in prison and her heart sank. Poor Jack. He was only trying to free the animals. *Sigh.* She tapped her pen on the table and tried to concentrate.

From her regular corner table at the Blind Faith Café, the chatter of other customers created a soothing soundtrack for her meditations on philosophy. The smell of carrot juice and tofu was reassuring, and the dimly lit booth was her own little cocoon. The bustling café helped ward off the loneliness of scholarly life.

She took a sip of her Witch's Brew tea, which her friend Amber insisted would "detox her liver chi and diffuse brain fog." Nope. Not today. She needed something stronger than roasted dandelion to part the clouds in her cranium. But four in the afternoon was probably too early for a Jack & Coke. *Sigh.* She thought of her mother sitting on the porch in her ratty recliner, drinking alone in the middle of the day. No way. She wasn't going to end up like her mom, living below the poverty line with only Vodka Collins and a litter box–challenged cat for company. Jessica would stick to tea, at least for now.

She focused her attention back on the screen. Her dissertation was on the influence of Nietzsche's philosophy on the Blue Rider artists, a forerunner to Expressionism founded by Russian emigrants and German artists in 1911. If she played her cards right, she could qualify for a job in either philosophy or art history. All she wanted was to be a teacher. Why did she have to write a book to get a job teaching? She slammed her computer shut and put her head in her hands.

She closed her eyes and plugged her ears, which only intensified the smell of burnt coffee and freshly baked bread. Banana nut pancakes, that's what she needed. She'd read on Facebook that bananas were brain food. She glanced around the café, looking for her waitress. Was her waitress the one with the blonde dreads and angel wings tattooed on her arms, or the one with the bleached buzz cut wearing a studded dog collar? The latter was two tables over, delivering a slice of carrot cake the size of Jessica's cowboy hat. She waved, but the waitress didn't see her. Instead, a dark-haired man waved back.

Crapulence! What is he doing here? For the last two years, she'd managed to avoid Nick Schilling, aka Professor Nicholas Charis . . . except for that one awkward departmental party where she'd spilled whiskey on his designer trousers and then tried to wipe it off. He hadn't wanted to rely on his father's prominence to get ahead in his field, so, years ago, he'd chosen to use his mother's maiden name professionally. His double life as wealthy art collector Nick Schilling and art history professor Nicholas Charis scared Jessica.

Two years ago, they'd had a really passionate—and really brief—relationship. She'd fallen in love with Nick Schilling and then discovered she needed Professor Nicholas Charis on her dissertation committee. Professor/student romance was a no-no. If the relationship continued, Nick's job wouldn't. She couldn't let him make that choice and ruin his career, so she'd made it for him and walked away. It was one of the hardest things she'd ever done.

Casually chic, as usual, Nick was wearing jeans, a black T-shirt, and a tailored designer jacket that suited his lean frame. But Nick Schilling's intense eyes belied his easy manner. There was a hard ambition lurking just under the surface of his effortless smile.

Her cheeks burned. *Why does he have to be so beautiful?* She opened her laptop, tapped it awake, and lowered her head until her nose almost touched the keyboard. Maybe he'd get the hint and go away.

No such luck.

"Dolce, I was hoping to run into you here." Nick's smile lit up his tan face. It belonged in a toothpaste commercial.

She cringed at the nickname. It had stuck to her like the Starbucks Cinnamon Dolce Frappuccino she'd ended up wearing the night she first met Nick at a poker game two years ago.

"I'm a regular." She glanced up from the keyboard and winced when he gazed down at her with those eyes as blue as the Montana sky. "How well you know me."

"I know there's nothing regular about you." He tilted his head to one side.

"Quit flirting. I need my degree more than I need you." A burning sensation in her chest told her that wasn't true. Choosing between dating Nick and spending the next decade chained to her computer, writing a boring dissertation on German philosophy, was a no-brainer—which is why her strategy when it came to him was avoidance. Otherwise, like a fresh batch of chocolate chip cookies, he was impossible to resist. But it wasn't cool to sleep with a member of your dissertation committee. So, Nick and her PhD were an either/or proposition.

"I'm not flirting, just stating facts." He had a mischievous glint in his eyes. "You are extraordinary, Jessica James."

Her mouth said, "Knock it off," but her heart said, *more, more, more.*

"How's your dissertation coming along? Are you ready to rock the world with your interpretation of the Blue Riders?" He pulled out a chair and sat across from her.

"It's going well," she lied.

"I have a proposal for you." His voice was as smooth as aged whiskey.

"Oh, yeah." Her stomach did a backflip. *Proposal or proposition?* She sat on her hands. Before she'd discovered his double life, she would have jumped at either.

"You've probably heard about the new Center for Russian Art and Culture we're opening downtown." He took off his jacket and slipped it over the back of the chair. "It's a museum loosely associated with the university."

Not a proposition or a proposal. *Dang.* She tightened her lips and tried not to look at his enticing forearms.

"My father donated the money," he said. She knew Nick's father was super rich, collected Russian art, and had come by his money through suspicious means. Nick had never wanted to talk about his father.

Nick pointed at the chair and she nodded. He sat down next to her. "He's trying to buy my love, as usual." When Nick tried to peek around her computer screen, she slammed it shut. "But that's none of your concern."

He gazed straight into her face, and she cursed those irritatingly perfect lips and adorable dimples.

"Dolce, I want you to be the assistant director. You'll be in on the ground floor, helping shape the museum."

She sat there, mouth open, gaping like a cut-throat trout pulled out of Whitefish Creek. Was he offering her a real job? Which Nick was making the offer? The playboy art collector or the hotshot art professor? Even after their intense, if brief, affair, and two years of watching him at a distance, he was still a mystery.

"But my dissertation—"

"I promise it won't interfere with your dissertation. In fact, you can use the Center to pursue your interest in Russian art." He steepled his fingers. "What better place to write about Kandinsky than in front of one of his masterpieces? We also have a Marianne von Werefkin self-portrait. You've got to come and see it."

Jessica squirmed in her chair. She'd love to see a Werefkin, one of the only women in the Blue Riders.

"And it will be great experience when you go on the job market next year. It's a real salary, not a graduate stipend." He was tapping his steepled forefingers together as if he was plotting something.

Her fellowship barely covered rent and one square a day. She really could use the money. "What's the job description? Would I be working for you?"

"You'd be working *with* me." His eyes lit up.

"Doing whatever you want me to do?" She reined in her imagination.

"Doing whatever you want. You would help with exhibits, education, outreach, everything. With your expertise, I know you'd contribute a lot to the Center. Who else in Chicago knows as much about Russian art as you?"

Flattery would get him everywhere. His citrus-and-juniper scent made her skin tingle. And the way he ran his fingers through his thick, wavy hair was deadly. She averted her eyes. Too late, the heat in her face betrayed her. "Can I think about it?" She tightened her lips to keep from smiling. She felt as if Nick could see inside her no matter how hard she tried to hide her feelings from him.

"Here are the terms." Nick pulled an envelope from his inside jacket pocket. He really had been looking for her. "Take your time. Think it over." His cheeks flushed. "If you like working at the Center, you could make a career of it."

Nick Schilling was always full of surprises. She thought of the time she'd worn his jacket to keep warm and had found a small handgun in the pocket.

The refrain from Beyoncé's "Daddy Lessons" chimed from across the table. "Excuse me," Nick said.

"My father." He pulled his phone from his pocket and flashed her an apologetic smile. "Hello," he said into the phone. The color drained from his face as if he'd been punched in the gut. "What? Who is this?" he demanded.

From across the table, Jessica watched the expressions on his face change as fast as thunderstorms moving across Lake Michigan. *What in the heck is going on?* Nick was usually as fresh as lettuce, but he was visibly upset by this call.

"My father." He dropped his phone onto the table and put his head in his hands. "He's dead." His chestnut hair fell over his fingers in waves of grief.

"I'm so sorry." Jessica scooted her chair next to his and put her hand on his arm.

When he twisted around and put his head on her shoulder, she had no choice but to put her arms around him. The warmth of his body made her shiver. She laid her head on top of his and thought of the day her own dad died. She was only ten. A blizzard had sent her home early from school. She was in the barn when she heard her mom wailing from the kitchen. The horrible sound had sent her into a panic and she hid. In some ways, she'd been hiding ever since.

Nick broke the hold and then pulled a pressed handkerchief from his breast pocket and blew his nose. "Will you come with me to his hotel?" he asked, red eyes pleading. "I can't face it alone."

What could she say? "Of course." She stuffed her

computer into her book bag, drained the dregs of her tea, and dropped a five-dollar bill on the table. "Let's go." Pancakes would have to wait. She'd lost her appetite anyway.

STOMACH GROWLING from too much detox tea and not enough food, Jessica followed Nick into the lobby of the Parker Hotel, a Chicago institution and one of the fanciest hotels downtown. The cavernous lobby was magnificent with its marble pillars and ornately carved wood-paneled ceiling. Towering ferns grew in gold pots, and a chandelier the size of a compact car hung above the registration desk. The lobby smelled of aged leather and high rollers. Legend had it that Al Capone wined and dined his ladies here in the famous High Mark restaurant. Nick had offered to take her there for dinner after the visit to his father's suite. She hugged herself to quiet her stomach. She could use some wining and dining, but the price of a free meal might be too high. Contrary to her mom's advice, she needed a career, not a sugar daddy.

A uniformed policeman met them at the registration desk and escorted them up to the suite. As soon as Jessica walked into the room, she smelled it: the sweet and sickening smell of Amber's homemade chamomile-lavender tea mixed with the hippie hacker's signature patchouli perfume. *Weird. Am I hallucinating?* No way her friend would be in this fancy hotel room with Nick's rich—dead—dad. Amber was one of Jessica's two closest friends: a Northwestern undergrad, a hobby hacker, an intern in the university's fundraising office, and a lover of all things New Age.

Jessica surveyed the suite, which was really more like an apartment with a wood-paneled study, a marble-floored foyer, and a posh living room. The elegant contemporary furniture was at odds with the rest of the baroque hotel. Her gaze homed in on a table in the dining room, upon which sat a silver room service tray with tea service for three. Nick's dad had entertained guests before he died, so where were those guests now? And why were there so many police officers in this hotel suite? *They must suspect Nick's father didn't die of natural causes.*

A slim woman officer waiting by the bedroom door gestured Nick inside. He glanced back at Jessica. She knew he wanted her to accompany him into the bedroom, but she just couldn't bring herself to do it. In her twenty-three years on the planet, she'd already seen two dead bodies and wasn't keen on seeing another. She shook her head. "I'll wait out here."

Nick took a deep breath and disappeared into the bedroom.

A paunchy policeman nodded to the woman officer. "Don't worry, Sergeant. I'll watch the girl."

They must suspect murder. Why else would I need watching? A cautious person might sit quietly on the couch, hands folded in their lap, demonstrating they were innocent as a baby. No watching necessary. Jessica wasn't that person. The paunchy policeman followed on Jessica's heels as she circled the dining room, focusing on the tea tray. No use trying to shake the cop. He was stuck on her like a deer tick. Trying to be inconspicuous, she glanced down at the teacups. One had purple lipstick on the rim, and all three held soggy, shriveled linen tea bags.

Those were Amber's homemade tea bags, alright. *But why would Amber, of all people, be having tea with Mr. Schilling?* Maybe it was part of her new job at the Development Office? Was she courting rich donors for the University now? Not likely, with her wild hair, buxom paisley dresses, and liberal use of the herbal calming tincture "Rescue Remedy."

Jessica slid the cell phone out of her fringe jacket pocket and snapped a picture to text Amber. She shielded the phone with her body so the cop couldn't see what she was doing.

"Who was here for tea?" Jessica asked the cop, trying to be nonchalant.

"That's what we're trying to find out." He grabbed her by the elbow and moved her a couple of feet away from the table—and the scene of the crime. "We think it was two women."

She rolled her eyes. "Unless Mr. Schilling wears—wore—purple lipstick." *And patchouli perfume*, she thought to herself. She could smell the pungent aroma lingering on a chair near the tea table. *Amber.* Definitely the hippie hacker's favorite scent.

"How'd he die?" Jessica asked in her sweetest voice, batting her eyelashes and smiling up at the policeman.

The policeman leaned closer and whispered, "Look, honey, the old duffer had a heart attack, so quit playing Sherlock Holmes." His breath smelled of garlic and spearmint.

She pulled out of his grip. "Heart attack?"

"Bad heart. Took medicine for it. Case closed." The cop seemed smug. "You his daughter-in-law?"

Her chest tightened. "No. Just a friend."

"Why don't you think it's a heart attack?" A woman's voice came from the bedroom. Was that the medical examiner? "I'll know more after the autopsy."

A familiar baritone boomed, "Gut instinct." She knew that voice. Detective Harvey Cormier. He'd been the lead detective on two other murder cases Jessica had somehow been mixed up in. He'd even saved her life once.

She knew it. The no-nonsense detective suspected foul play. Amber might have been the last one to see Mr. Schilling alive . . . and therefore was the prime suspect. Detective Cormier's gut was usually right. He was a gem of a cop—one who genuinely cared about people and wanted to make the world a better place.

When the uniformed cop turned around to greet his boss, Jessica scooted over to the table, snatched one soggy tea bag, and sunk it into her jacket pocket. She glanced around. The officer was standing at attention, blocking the detective's view. She quickly pulled a tissue from her other pocket, wiped the handle of the cup with the lipstick on it, and then smeared the lipstick until it disappeared. Now at least it would take the cops a bit longer to link Amber to the crime . . . time she needed to find out who really killed Nick's dad. She stepped away from the table and tried to look innocent.

Jessica couldn't believe she was getting involved with another murder investigation. She had her dissertation to write, and she didn't need the distraction—no matter how much she may have wanted one an hour ago. But Amber was one of her best friends, and she knew even good detectives like Harvey Cormier sometimes let misleading evidence take them down the wrong trail. She couldn't let that happen to Amber.

"But, if you'll approve an autopsy, we'll know for sure." Cormier's bass voice was getting closer.

Jessica swung around.

Detective Cormier raised his eyebrows when he saw her. "Miss James." The deep buzzing of his voice reminded her of an electric razor. No way Chicago's chief homicide detective would be at the scene unless it was murder.

In spite of her wool socks and cowboy boots, Jessica's feet broke out in a cold sweat. She buttoned her jacket against the blasting air-conditioning. Either Nick's father ran hot or the police were keeping the hotel suite extra cold to preserve the dead body. Chills raced up her spine just thinking about the corpse in the next room.

She took another look around the suite, trying to memorize every detail. The lights of Chicago's skyline glowed through the closed sheer curtains. The morning paper sat unread on an end table, next to an ashtray streaked with ashes but no butts. On the coffee table, a basket of fruit wrapped in cellophane suggested Mr. Schilling had checked in recently—either that or he didn't eat fruit. Maybe he was on one of those low-sugar diets. Jessica glanced back at the table and tea service. A half-eaten cookie shot down her diet theory. Unless the perp had taken a bite before poisoning her victim . . . Jessica inhaled, imprinting the smell of chamomile-lavender on her brain for future reference.

"Collect those cups and dishes. I'll have them checked for chemicals," Detective Cormier pointed at the tea tray. A uniformed officer wearing blue latex gloves sealed the dishes in bags and arranged them in a cardboard box.

"Was Mr. Schilling murdered?" Jessica asked the detective. Given the three cops in the suite, creating a diversion and stealing more evidence wasn't an option.

"At this point, we're investigating every angle." Detective Cormier gestured toward the sitting area. "It looks like natural causes, but something's just not right." The detective turned to Nick, who had just walked out of the bedroom, still shaken, his face pale, his gait unsteady. "Do you have a minute?" It was more of a statement than a question. "I'd like to ask you a few questions."

Nick nodded and took a seat on the sofa. The red capillaries surrounding his irises made the blue of his eyes even more intense, and the black stubble on his chin stood out against his wan complexion. Poor guy looked awful. She wanted to stroke his stubbly cheek. He glanced over at Jessica and patted the cushion next to him. She obliged.

"When was the last time you saw your father?" the detective asked. "Alive," he added.

"Last year in New York. To get me to attend his wedding, he lured me there with promises of funding the new Center for Russian Art." Nick stared down at his hands, which were folded in his lap.

"You haven't seen your father in a year?" The detective sounded surprised.

"Not every family is close, Detective Cormier." Nick fiddled with a crested gold ring on his pinky finger.

Tell me about it, Jessica thought. *And not every father is what he seems.* She knew that from her own experience, although she knew she could be jumping to conclusions about Nick's dad.

"Dad wrote to me a few days ago. He said he had a surprise for me. He hinted it was rubies and diamonds or something." Nick sighed.

"You have no idea what he wanted?"

Nick shook his head.

"Can you confirm your father's full name is Richard Weinhaus Schilling?"

"Yes."

"And his home address is Westchester County, New York."

"Yes."

"Why was your father in Chicago?" Cormier asked. The way his crisp linen shirt hugged his muscular torso, along with his flawless skin, angled jaw, and close-cropped dark hair made him look more like a Caribbean crooner than a homicide detective.

"For the grand opening of the Center." Nick twisted his ring.

"Tell me about this center."

"The new Center for Russian Art and Culture." Nick glanced over at Jessica. "My father put up the funds to build it. It is connected with the university but run separately."

"I see." Detective Cormier raised his eyebrows. "Did your father leave a will?"

"I assume he did." Nick glanced up from troubling his ring.

"Do you have any siblings?"

"No."

"So, you're the primary beneficiary?" Detective Cormier aimed his penetrating gaze at Nick's face.

"I wouldn't make that assumption," Nick said without blinking.

The detective scribbled something on his notepad.

"Did your father have any health issues? Was he depressed?"

"Depressed? No. My father was the kind of seventy-year-old who gets younger with age. Just over a year ago, he returned from a Bali honeymoon with his twenty-eight-year-old bride, Chrissy, a Victoria's Secret model. I'm pretty sure he didn't kill himself."

"You think this new wife might have murdered him for his money?" Jessica asked. "In murder mysteries, it's always the wife."

"Knowing my father, he made her sign a prenup like he did his last three wives. No one was getting their hands on his fortune." Nick rubbed his face. For the first time, Jessica noticed the purple bags beneath his eyes.

"But a prenup isn't the same as a will—"

"We'll follow up with the wife," the detective interrupted her. "Now, about his heart—he was taking digitalis?"

"Yes. I believe so." Nick stared down at his hands.

"Could he have taken an overdose?"

"One pill too many," Jessica whispered.

"I don't know." Nick glanced up at the detective.

Detective Cormier pulled latex gloves from his pocket and snapped them on. "Sergeant, bring me the envelope." He pointed to the box of evidence the other cops had been collecting.

The police woman handed Cormier a large white envelope sealed in a giant baggie. He carefully opened the plastic bag and removed the envelope. "Have you seen this before?" The detective held it out so Nick could see it. "Please don't touch it."

Jessica leaned forward to look at it. "It's from the University."

The detective nodded. "Something called the *Development Office*, which must be in charge of fundraising."

"I don't know. Maybe it's the paperwork related to my father's donation?" Nick went to take the envelope, but Cormier pulled it back.

The detective slipped the envelope back into the baggie. "It contains signed documents leaving his entire Russian art collection to the Center for Russian Art and Culture, along with another two million dollars, which, if I read the fine print correctly, is earmarked for Russian refugees living in Chicago."

Nick's eyes widened. "What?"

"Are you planning to expand your Center to serve refugees?"

"No. I don't know anything about this." Nick shook his head. "Frankly, I'm completely baffled."

Jessica stifled a gasp. *Amber!* She volunteered at a refugee services center. And she worked at the Development Office. And her weird herbal tea bags were in the room service cups. Jessica had to get to her friend before the cops did.

2

Detective Cormier stretched his smooth brown arm across the open hotel elevator door, keeping it from closing. Jessica and Nick faced him from inside. "Professor, we may want to ask you some more questions. It would be helpful if you stayed in town." Cormier glanced at Jessica. "Miss James, good to see you again," he said with a smile. "I'm sure a possible murder mystery will keep *you* in town."

She cringed. Was she getting a reputation with the Chicago homicide unit? True, trouble seemed to follow her. But it was never her fault—well, hardly ever. This time, for sure, it wasn't. She'd never even met Nick's father, and now she never would.

"Am I a suspect?" Nick asked. "Good lord. My father's lying in there dead—" He put his head in his hands.

"No, Professor," Detective Cormier said in a reassuring voice.

But something in his tone told Jessica he did suspect Nick. She knew the detective well enough to know there was something he wasn't saying.

Detective Cormier held out a business card. "Call me if you think of anything that might shed light on your father's death."

Nick's hand trembled as he took the card. "Please call me as soon as you get the autopsy report. I want to know how he died." He looked ten years older than he did an hour ago.

"Poison," Jessica said under her breath. "Someone poisoned him," she said louder, then bit her cuticle.

"Perhaps." The detective took his hand away from the elevator door.

"Poison!" Nick exclaimed as the doors shut. "Why do you say that?"

"Well, I won't be surprised if it turns out to be poison."

"You've been reading too many detective stories instead of writing your dissertation." He leaned against the wall of the elevator.

Maybe Nick was right. She'd been involved with too many murders recently, and now she was seeing them everywhere. "Guilty as charged." She stared up at the illuminated numbers. She knew if she looked at Nick, she wouldn't be able to resist touching him. Anyway, she had a boyfriend, didn't she?

Again, she thought of poor Jack stuck in prison. It wasn't like she was in a *relationship* with him. They'd only kissed once, right before he'd been busted for liberating the animals at the research hospital last year. Really, they were just friends, really good friends. She glanced over at Nick and guilt wrapped its grubby paws around her innards and squeezed. Her sort-of-boyfriend was in prison because of her. Why had she asked him to free the poor chimp from the research lab? And here she was fantasizing about another man. Now wasn't the time to think of romance . . . with Nick *or* Jack. She'd just been in a suite with a dead body, for God's sake.

She pulled her phone from her jacket pocket, tapped it awake, and called Amber. Instant voice mail. Amber had her phone off. Thumbs flying, she sent her friend a text message: *Call me!* She had to find out how Amber's tea bags had ended up in the dead man's cups.

Her phone beeped, indicating she had her own voice mail waiting. She clicked and . . . *Wait. What?* Jack had called. *Crapulence!* He'd used his precious minutes on his super-expensive inmate phone card. She glanced over at Nick while she listened to the message. Another twinge of guilt pinched her heart when Jack signed off with "I love you, cowgirl." Every time he said it, she cringed. She never knew how to answer. Usually, she just said, "I know. Me too."

"What's wrong?" Nick asked. "You look like you've seen a ghost."

"It's nothing," Jessica lied. Nick was dealing with his own ghosts—all too fresh. She didn't need to resurrect her own.

"Are you hungry?" Nick asked. "I don't have an appetite, but I could use a drink."

Like most starving grad students, Jessica never turned down free food or drink. "Me too." Eating always cheered her up. Maybe it would take her mind off poor Jack, rotting in that prison cell . . . and her appetite for Nick.

When Nick put his hand on the small of her back, a jolt of electricity rushed up her spine. *Damn!* With Jack, it was a slow burn, but with Nick, it was a spontaneous combustion. Her heart was playing tug-of-war with her brain.

Nick led her into the restaurant. With its crystal chandeliers, satin chairs, carved wooden tables, and patrons dressed in fancy evening wear, the place reminded her of the dinner scene on the Titanic, right before it sank. In her scuffed red cowboy boots, balding suede jacket, and faded jeans, she was severely underdressed.

The hostess seemed to know Nick—either that or she wanted to get to know him. She was very friendly as she led them to a table in the corner.

Candlelight, a jazz pianist, a single rose in a cut glass vase—under other circumstances, it would have been very romantic. But with Nick's father lying dead on the fifth floor and her dream of getting a PhD on its last legs, the dinner felt more like a wake.

Nick ordered a neat single-malt scotch with a name she couldn't pronounce. She was tempted to get her usual Jack & Coke, but decided on a cosmopolitan instead. More sophisticated.

She scanned the menu for vegetarian options. Well, it wasn't going to take her long to decide. There was only one—pasta with kohlrabi, rocket, and blood orange reduction. Sounded more like a homicide at the International Space Station than a meal.

Nick ordered a bowl of Moroccan soup.

"That's all you're having?" she asked.

In answer, he held up his empty glass and ordered another Lagavulin.

"Tell me about your dad," she said, avoiding eye contact.

Nick made a weird snorting sound. "My dad." He shut his eyes. "He always bragged he was a 'self-made man.' Grew up on the streets of the Bronx and died in a penthouse suite." He twisted the ring on his little finger as his refill arrived.

"So, he wasn't always wealthy?" Jessica asked.

"No. He hustled his way to the top in New York real estate and then bought a couple of nightclubs, a coal mine, and a casino." Nick chuckled again. "He bragged about his street smarts and belittled my book learning."

"He didn't want you to become a professor?" she asked.

"He didn't want me, full stop." Nick downed his scotch and signaled the waiter for another.

She shifted in her chair. She could relate. She always thought her dad wished she'd been a boy. She gulped down her drink. "Do you think his new wife might have had something to do with his death?" She couldn't bring herself to say *murder*.

"Chrissy?" Nick's eyes flashed. "Who knows? She's a schemer." He shook his head. "But a killer? Hard to believe."

"Why isn't she here with your dad?"

"Probably on a catwalk in Paris or Rome." Nick arched his brows and sipped the drink that had just arrived. "She usually travels without Dad. I suspect that's not all she does without him, if you know what I mean."

Yes, I do. She stared at the napkin in her lap. She couldn't help it. As much as she tried to purge her feelings for Nick, she couldn't. Seeing him this vulnerable was like pouring gasoline on the burning embers of her heart.

"What's wrong, Dolce?" he asked.

Jessica pushed a rocket (aka arugula) leaf around her plate with her fork. When she glanced up, her eyes met his. She jumped up from the table to avoid bursting into tears. She must have looked a mess, because she didn't even have to ask—a waiter pointed her to the bathroom. *Pull yourself together, cowgirl.* Must be PMS. She wasn't usually this emotional. Or maybe it was sitting across from Nick Schilling. She wanted him. She might even love him. She felt like she might barf.

When she returned to the table, Nick was sporting another full glass of whiskey. Was that his fourth? She was getting worried. It was barely two in the afternoon.

"Are you okay?" Nick asked.

"Just thinking about your dad," she lied. "What was his interest in the Center?"

"At first, I thought he was trying to reconcile with me." He fiddled with his ring. "Then last week one of his business associates showed up giving me instructions on my dad's paintings: which to sell, which to keep, and how the money would be split. I started to wonder . . ." He took another sip of whiskey and then glanced at his fancy wristwatch. "I've got to get back to the Center." He sat his glass down on the table. "Would you like to come along? I could show you around and introduce you to the staff." He smiled. "The job offer's still on the table." He patted the tablecloth for emphasis.

She nodded and finished her Cosmo.

"Do you mind driving?" He handed her a Porsche key fob. "I may have had a wee bit too much scotch."

Ten minutes later, cruising down Lake Shore Drive, weaving in and out of traffic, she glanced over at Nick. He forced a sickly smile. The Porsche was itchin' to break the wimpy 45 mph speed limit on this poor excuse for an expressway. She missed the wide-open freeway in Montana, where the speed limit was 75 and even the farmers in their pickup trucks did 80.

"Take the Touhy exit up ahead," Nick said. "That's it on the right." He pointed. "The one with the stained glass window."

"Oh my god. That's beautiful." She couldn't believe her eyes. "You built that?"

"Well, I didn't actually build it."

"You know what I mean."

The building was a cross between a Gothic church and a Spanish Colonial townhouse in the French Quarter of New Orleans. At one end, there was a stunning stained glass window framed by ornate stone, and at the other, a white stucco building with wrought iron balconies and a red tile roof. The two sides of the building were at war. She'd never seen anything like it.

"I love it," she said as she pulled the Porsche into the side parking lot.

An expansive concrete stairway with fanning metal handrails and a wheelchair ramp lead to the entrance of the Center.

Nick opened one of the two glass doors and she scooted inside.

"Wow!" She gawked at the polished wood floors and then up at the ceiling two stories overhead.

If on the outside, the Center for Russian Art and Culture looked like an eighteenth-century convent meets Bourbon Street, on the inside, it was futuristic glass and steel.

"Come on," Nick said. "I'll show you the offices and introduce you, and then we can take a tour of the collection."

"Amazing." In a daze, she followed him through the foyer and down a side hallway. The tap of her boots across the floor echoed through the building. She felt like she'd been shushed by an invisible librarian. Embarrassed, she tried to walk on her toes.

Along the corridor, there were four glass doors. Only one of them was open. Jessica stopped in her tracks when she saw a familiar hunched silhouette through the opaque glass: Dmitry Durchenko, Lolita's dad. The philosophy department's brooding janitor always seemed to be hiding from something. *What is he doing here?*

3

Dmitry Durchenko refolded the letter and put it back in its envelope. A tapping in the hall caught his attention, and he glanced up just in time to see Mr. Nick with that friend of Lolita's, the pretty blonde girl—Jessica. He hoped Mr. Nick and Jessica weren't back together again. Last time, it nearly cost the poor girl her life.

Dmitry put the letter into the pocket of his linen jacket and patted his pocket for safekeeping. It wasn't every day he got a letter from his mother telling him to expect a visit all the way from Moscow. He tugged at his shirt collar, which was suddenly too tight around this throat. She wanted to talk to him about Sergei's death. *Why now? Did she find out Father had ordered him killed?*

The last time he saw his older brother was twenty-two years ago, at the abandoned hospital on the outskirts of Moscow. The memory attacked unbidden, as usual. His father commanding him to make the kill . . . his brother tied up in the trunk of a car, face bloodied beyond recognition, just before he was shot. There'd been no love lost between Dmitry and his brother, but even Sergei hadn't deserved to be executed for stealing from Bratva. He should have known better. The Russian mafia didn't tolerate thieves or snitches.

Dmitry straightened some papers on his desk and tried to shake the traumatic memory from his mind. His father was dead. His brother was dead. His life in Bratva was long behind him. He needed to let it go. His wife and daughter were safe, and so was he. He didn't have to keep looking over his shoulder. He'd made a new life for himself. There was nothing to worry about. So why was he sweating?

He wiped his brow with a handkerchief. He would see his mother in less than a week. Leaving her before his twentieth birthday had been the hardest part of escaping a life of crime. She hadn't wanted that life for him anymore than he'd wanted it for himself. She'd helped plan his departure. She was the one who'd stolen the money and the paintings. At least his father never found out she was the culprit. If he had, she'd have been the next mark taken out to the abandoned hospital.

His cell phone buzzing interrupted his thoughts. It was Lolita. His mood lightened.

"*Kotyonok*, I just received a letter from your grandmother." He pressed the button for speakerphone so he could hear better. "She's coming to visit."

"I know. She called me." Lolita's silky voice was a tonic for his nerves.

"Of course. You talk to her more than I do." Ever since Lolita met her grandmother and namesake two years ago, they'd been thick as thieves. At twenty-one, his daughter looked exactly like his mother had when he'd left Russia. The resemblance was uncanny. No wonder they'd hit it off.

"She's thinking of moving to Chicago so we can see her all the time. Wouldn't that be great?" She sounded so happy.

"Yes, *kotyonok,* it would."

"Dad, you know I don't like you to call me *kitten*."

"Why don't you stop by tonight?" He changed the subject. "Your mother misses you."

"I'm busy with schoolwork. I'll visit next weekend."

She always said 'next weekend.' Why didn't she visit more often? He'd always thought they were a close-knit family, just the three of them. But lately, his daughter was always too busy.

"You aren't hosting those illegal poker games again?"

"Dad, don't worry about me." She sighed into the phone. "I can take care of myself."

"I know." He'd made sure she could take care of herself. As soon as she could walk, he'd started teaching her martial arts. He never knew when Bratva would find him—or worse, her—and he wanted to be ready. "How about I take you out for an ice cream. I can come by campus on my way home."

"Ice cream!" She laughed. "Do you think I'm five years old?"

"Okay, how about vodka and *salo* at Pavlov's?" Pavlov's Banquet was one of her favorite hangouts. They used to go there as a family to get the best Russian food in Chicago, which was pretty good. But, his wife's, Sabina's, cooking was better. But growing up, Lolita loved to go to Pavlov's.

"When grandma gets here, we can go to Pavlov's. I've got to go now, Dad."

"When grandma gets here," he repeated, but she'd already hung up.

What will become of Lolita? She was at the top of her class at Northwestern, but she always wanted more. He'd scrubbed toilets to barely afford her tuition, but she always seemed to have money to spare from her poker games. She was tough as nails but vulnerable as a kitten. As hard as he tried, he didn't understand his daughter. Maybe she was too American.

Laughing sounds from Mr. Nick's office next door brought Dmitry back, and he glanced at the wall clock. Soon he'd be home with Sabina, and then he could relax and forget. He tidied up his desk, straightening the corner of a notebook, organizing the pencils and pens in the cup according to height, setting the tape dispenser parallel to the stapler. When everything was just right, he removed his handkerchief from his breast pocket and wiped the wooden surface of the desk. *Old habits die hard.*

Sometimes he missed cleaning Brentano Hall at the University, the smells of wood polish and centuries-old cigar smoke hanging onto the wainscoting. The old Victorian house was nothing like the Center, where everything smelled new and rich, with a hint of that perfume Mr. Nick always wore.

At least now he could hold his head up. For the last two weeks, he wasn't a janitor anymore. He had an important job working for Mr. Nick at the new Center for Russian Art and Culture, and, except for his family, there was nothing Dmitry loved more than Russian art. He remembered the day his father bought Kandinsky's *Composition VII*. That painting was burnt into his brain with the force of a branding iron. He'd only been a boy, but the vibrant colors sent his heart soaring. That's when he knew he wanted to be a painter. Of course, life had other plans . . . and so had his father.

Dmitry stood up, brushed lint off his new slacks, and then took his hat from the coat rack. He was just angling it on his head when a man appeared in the doorway. The bearded face was familiar, but Dmitry couldn't place him. He narrowed his eyes at the uncanny stranger. He'd just been thinking about his brother, and now he was hallucinating him alive again. He shuddered.

Maybe Sabina was right and he should see a therapist. But talking about his feelings wasn't going to exorcise the demons from his past. Even a priest couldn't help him. He was beyond redemption. Mother Russia was both his salvation and his damnation. He couldn't go back, but he couldn't be rid of her either. Twenty-three years was a long time to be haunted by a country and a brother who now lived only in his imagination. He blinked. The uncanny stranger was still there, standing in the doorway, smiling.

"Long time no see, brother," the man said in Russian.

The voice was like a Taser to the ribs. It was a voice Dmitry thought he'd never hear again in his life. But there was no doubt about it. He'd know that voice anywhere.

"Sergei." Dmitry exhaled his older brother's name like a sigh of exhaustion. He needed to sit down. This was like seeing a ghost. The weight of it bore down on him and he slumped back into his chair. As his mother would say, "flies got caught in the web when hornets went free."

"Let me guess, *brother*," Sergei spat out the word. "You thought I was dead."

When he laughed, Dmitry saw something sinister in his brother's eyes—the same look he'd seen hundreds of times growing up, watching Sergei torture insects and rodents for kicks. *How is this possible?* He'd heard rumors Sergei had escaped. And then that Olga woman had shown him a picture of a man who could have been

Sergei. Of course, the man in the trunk had been beaten so badly he was unrecognizable. But Dmitry had been sure it was Sergei, and Dmitry had heard the shots.

Why would Father's Vory *let Sergei go free? And where was he hiding all this time?* All these questions ran through Dmitry's mind, but all he could say was, "What do you want? Why are you here?" God knew he wasn't exactly happy to see his brother again. Sergei had bullied him all through their childhood. Why would he be glad to see him again now? Especially after he betrayed Dmitry and his mother. Even if his father had been a nasty piece of work, he'd taught Dmitry the importance of loyalty.

"Is that any way to talk to your brother?" Sergei continued in Russian.

"My brother died in that hospital," Dmitry said in English. "You're not my brother."

Sergei laughed again, this time a big belly laugh that made his eyes spark and his mustache twitch. "That's right, you're not my brother. You're just the bastard child of our mother's infidelity. I'm the one true heir to the Yudkovich dynasty." An aching insecurity lurked behind his boisterous laughter and hard demeanor, and that's what made him so dangerous.

"Is that why you're here? The inheritance?" Dmitry shook his head. "You'll have to take that up with Mom. She inherited the *dynasty*." Anton Yudkovich had expected his son to join the family business and eventually take over Bratva. Thanks to his mother's help,

Dmitry had escaped a life of crime, made his way to the states, and changed his name to *Durchenko*, Sabina's family name.

"I think we're having translation problems," Sergei said as he stepped into the office and shut the door. "Father's true legacy is not his money or his stupid art collection. It's his business."

"I don't know anything about his 'business,' if that's what you want to call it." Dmitry clenched his fists.

"I think you do, brother." Sergei strolled across the room and stopped in front of the desk. "You know a lot more than you let on."

Being this close to his brother after all these years was unnerving. Dmitry removed his hat and slumped against the back of the chair. "I don't want anything to do with the business. That's why I left Moscow, to get out once and for all."

"You can't get out. You'll never get out. It's in your blood." Sergei sat on the edge of the desk and lit a cigar. He puffed a couple times to get it going and then blew a big cloud into Dmitry's face. "Oh, I forgot. You don't have my father's blood in your veins. You are the son of that weakling Count Volkov." He laughed. "You didn't think I knew that, did you?"

Dmitry closed his eyes. How was he going to get out of this situation? Sabina would be wondering where he was. *Blyad!* His wife would go through the roof when she heard Sergei was alive and well and in Chicago.

What in the hell is he doing here? And what does he want? Whatever it was, Dmitry didn't want to give it.

"My father disowned me and cut me out of his will. He ordered my execution, for God's sake. And our mother won't speak to me. So, I have no choice but to take what's rightfully mine from you, dear brother." Sergei stroked his beard.

Dmitry pushed his chair back to escape the cloud of cigar smoke. There was really nowhere else to go. His brother had him cornered like an animal. It was just like the old days, plus a good twenty pounds and a big bushy beard. With the extra weight and the cigar, Sergei looked exactly like his father—craggy face, Brillo-pad hair, and sausage fingers.

"Cheer up, brother," Sergei said, his cigar between his teeth. "I come with an offer."

Dmitry merely sighed. He should have known. A real job. It was too good to be true. No matter how fast he ran, he was never going to outrun the past. Dmitry closed his eyes and waved his hat in the air, as if he had the power to cast out his brother with his gesture.

"You haven't even heard the offer yet." Sergei stubbed his cigar out on the desk and put the butt in the pocket of his wrinkled suit jacket. "You'll like it."

"Wanna bet?" Dmitry asked. Even as a kid, his brother had loved to gamble. He'd challenge Dmitry to bet him who could hold their breath the longest, who could eat the most tea cakes, who could pee the furthest. Whatever the contest, Sergei always won. But he wasn't going to win this time.

"I've just taken over the Chicago territory, filling in for the Pope after his untimely demise." Sergei's crooked smile sent tremors down Dmitry's spine. "We need you. You're family. Speaking of family, I'm impressed with Lolita. You've done a good job raising my niece."

When Sergei mentioned his daughter's name, Dmitry cringed. Inhaling and exhaling like a bull about to charge, he balled up his fists. "Leave her out of this."

"Oh, but I can't, brother." Sergei stood up and came around the desk until he was so close Dmitry could feel his breath. "That's the beauty of it."

Dmitry tightened his lips. He felt like punching his brother in the mouth. But he knew that would only land him in a world of hurt.

"She's a gorgeous girl. You must be proud of her." Sergei winked. "And so enterprising too. Her poker games are legendary. Even Bratva wants a cut of those babies."

"Lolita is out of the poker business. She's nobody." Dmitry wondered if getting on his knees and begging would make a difference. "She's just a student finishing her college degree. Leave her be." *What does he want? Why show up now?* Dmitry's head was spinning.

"That's up to you, brother." Sergei spit out the words. "I have a job for you. You do it and you'll never see me again. That's what you want, isn't it?"

It was true. At this moment, Dmitry wanted nothing more than to never see his brother again. He wished he could make Sergei disappear, along with their whole sordid past. "What kind of job?"

"You do this one job, no questions—just follow my orders—and you and Lolita will never see me again." Sergei sounded exactly like his father had when he ordered him to "do this one job" out at the abandoned hospital, a job Dmitry wished he had done so he wouldn't be facing his brother again now.

"You've seen Lolita?" He tugged at his shirt collar.

"Why wouldn't I visit my niece? She's even more beautiful than Sabina." Sergei smirked. "How is Sabina?"

He shuddered at the mention of his wife's name. "Let's get this over with." Dmitry folded his arms over his chest. "What do you want from me?" *I should have killed you when I had the chance*, he thought and balled up his fists.

"I asked you a question. How is your wife?"

"What are you playing at?" Dmitry narrowed his brows. "Sabina's fine." He hoped he was right.

"Are you sure, brother?" Sergei grinned. "When was the last time you saw her?"

4

Nick Schilling sat on the edge of his desk so he could be closer to Dolce. She seemed uneasy sitting in the upholstered chair in his office. She was fiddling with the fringe on her jacket, her eyes darting around the room. He hoped she approved of what she saw.

He'd spent days picking out just the right furnishings to make his office perfect— stately slate-gray chairs, a black-and-gray French rug in the middle of the bamboo floor, and a sleek steel desk. He was going for an elegant, clean look, complimented by Alexey Titarenko's stark and haunting black-and-white photographs of St. Petersburg hanging on the walls. These days, there was nowhere he'd rather be than at his office. And having Dolce with him made it even sweeter.

Still, he felt numb. His dad had just died. Why

didn't he feel anything? His stomach soured remembering his father's dead face. The ashen death mask had resembled his father, but somehow that corpse lying on the bed wasn't his father. He couldn't explain it. Maybe because he'd lost his father long ago, when he'd become a "lowly" art history professor. Even as a child, Nick had been weak. An embarrassment of a son.

Nick pushed the thoughts of the dead man out of his mind. After all, he was with the woman he loved, and maybe that was enough.

"Detective Cormier thinks your dad was murdered." Jessica bit her fingernail. "What do you think?"

"I don't know what to think." He ran his hand through his hair. "I don't talk to him for years, then he wants to donate to the Center, and now he's dead."

"Maybe his new wife didn't want him to donate. Maybe she wanted it all." She wiped her hands on her jeans.

"Chrissy? She's conniving enough, but I'm not sure she's evil." He twisted the class ring on his little finger.

A knock at the door startled him. He'd been so intent on staring into Jessica's endless blue eyes.

The perky intern, Sally Marshall, peeked her head in. "I hope I'm not interrupting?" She glared at Jessica.

"I'd better get back to my writing." Jessica shifted in the chair. "I should go."

"Can you come back in a few minutes, Sally?" Why had she turned up now? The pesky intern was starting to annoy him. When she'd gone, he turned back to

Jessica. "Dolce, please stay just a bit longer." He realized he must sound like he was begging.

"Don't call me that." Jessica scrunched her brows.

"Sorry." He couldn't help thinking of her as *dolce*, sweet. He'd tried to forget about her by using online dating sites known for awkward lunches and discretion. But after two years of trying to find common ground with uptight curators and needy businesswomen, he'd given up. "Jessica," he whispered. Just saying her name filled him with longing.

"Are you okay?" she asked as she got up from the chair.

No, no he wasn't okay . . . not without her. No matter how beautiful or sexy or smart, at some point, he couldn't help comparing every other woman to her. He nodded. "I'll be fine."

"Thanks for showing me around," she said, buttoning her jacket.

He couldn't understand why she wore that grungy old cowhide, but somehow it made him love her even more. He got up and went to her side. He took her arm. "Thank you for coming with me to see my . . . to the Parker. And don't forget about the job offer."

Dolce blushed. He shouldn't have mentioned the job offer at a time like this.

She jerked away and headed for the door. He opened it for her and followed her out into the hall. "I don't know how I could have faced it without you."

"Are you sure you're going to be okay?" When she

turned around and gazed up at him with her face fresh with freckles, he dug his nails into his palms until it hurt.

"Don't worry about me." He reached down and brushed a strand of hair from her face. He knew he shouldn't have, but he couldn't help it. "Can I give you a lift?"

"No. I'd rather take the train." She wrinkled her brows and pulled away. "It's back to the salt mines for me." Her smile seemed forced. "See you around."

She turned to go. He was desperate for the magic words to make her stay. But all he could blurt out was, "Can I at least give you cab fare?"

She shook her head and picked up her pace.

What an idiot! 'Can I give you cab fare?' He stood frozen, watching her clicking away in those ridiculously endearing red boots. He called after her, "Remember my offer. You're perfect for the job." He believed it, but he couldn't trust himself. After all, he wasn't impartial. Was he offering her the position because of her intelligence and talent? Or because he wanted her close by?

Whichever the case, it didn't matter. He was sure she wouldn't take it. She'd made it pretty clear she wanted nothing to do with him romantically. Strictly professional, that's how he would play it. He'd promised her when they broke up two years ago. And, more to the point, he'd promised himself. He'd been taken off guard by the intensity of his feelings and he'd promised himself to regain his composure. Then there was the matter of the faculty handbook and its new rules. These days, brushing that hair from her face could actually cost him his job.

Maybe the job was the problem. If he just quit, then all the rules of their relationship would change. Of course, that was a reason not to hire her at the Center. He didn't want their relationship to remain strictly business. He wanted a full partnership, personal and professional.

He inhaled the scent of new construction, fresh paint and floor glue, and headed back to his office. He needed to think, and he didn't want to go back home. Not yet. Not alone.

He was startled by a well-dressed bearded man in the corridor. The stranger gave him a polite nod, and Nick moved to let him pass. He watched the man adjust his hat as he strolled toward the exit. The hairs on his arms stood on end as though a cold breeze had just blown past.

When the man was out of sight, Nick turned back and continued down the hallway, not knowing what else to do. He wondered if he had any more little bottles of scotch in his desk drawer. He collected them on flights from France, Germany, and Russia. Flying first class had its advantages. Luckily, he didn't have to make those trips on his measly professor's salary. Teaching was just something to do, something to keep him off the streets. Why not quit? Especially now that he had the

Center. If he quit, maybe he could have Jessica *and* the Center. What more could he want?

He quickened his pace. There must be at least one more tiny whiskey left from last week's flight back from Paris.

When he saw a light on in one of the offices, he went to investigate. "What are you still doing here, my friend?"

Dmitry Durchenko glanced up from his desk. He looked more like a man in his sixties than his forties. "I'm just finishing up." A shadow fell across Dmitry's face. The moody Russian was always hard to read, but something was wrong. Even his posture was off.

"Why don't we go get a drink?" Nick asked.

"Sorry, I can't." Dmitry pushed his chair back and stood up. "I have to get home." He picked a piece of lint from the sleeve of his jacket. "Sabina will be worried."

"Another time, then," Nick said, wondering what it must be like to have a devoted wife waiting at home.

"Yes, another time." When Dmitry took his raincoat from the coat rack, his hand shook.

"Are you ill?" Nick asked. "You look like you've seen a specter."

"I have." Dmitry slipped past Nick and strode down the hall.

What the hell is wrong with him? As he returned to his own office, Nick wondered if it had something to do with the bearded man.

At the doorway, Nick gaped at his office like he'd

never seen it before. Suddenly it seemed sparse and cold. He shivered and flipped off the fluorescent lights. In the darkness, he made his way to his desk. By memory, he opened the top drawer and felt around for his airplane plunder. *Thank God.* He pulled all three tiny bottles out of the drawer. He lined them up on the desk. He unscrewed each cap and dropped them, one by one, into the empty wastebasket. *Ting. Ting. Ting.* He sucked down one whiskey and chucked the bottle, then did the same with the second and third.

He tapped his phone. When it flickered to life, the image of his father's ashen face flashed into his mind. Who wanted him dead? Once he started counting, he realized the list was long: Chrissy, his "business associates," the mob, Victor "Teeth" Marsiano (his father's best "business" buddy and mobster), and more. The question was, who didn't want him dead? Poisoning didn't really seem like Victor's game. And Chrissy was too much of an airhead to pull off a murder.

Nick exhaled out loud. His ribs hurt like they were caught in a vice. He needed some distraction, something to make him feel alive again, something to fill the void. He quickly tapped the Tinder icon and scrolled through his messages, dozens of messages and most of them old. He hadn't been on here in a while . . . not since his last date, when he opened one eye to watch the woman silently gathering her clothes and sneaking out of his apartment with morning-after remorse written all over her face. He'd seen it many times, sometimes in his own bathroom mirror. He opened the most recent message. Brittany, twenty-five years old. In her profile photo, she was smiling with her finger posed to look like she was toppling the Eiffel Tower in the distance. *Oh, what the hell.* Nick typed, "Want to grab a drink?"

While waiting for Brittany to respond, he flipped through other photos, swiping left or right without thinking. One face made him stop. His finger hovering over the screen, he took a closer look. Must be the whiskey. For a second, he thought it was Jessica. He flipped his phone face-down on his desk and buried his face in his hands.

5

Jessica slung her jacket over her shoulder and boarded the elevated train. The train car was jam-packed with commuters heading back to the Chicago suburbs. Bodies jostled against her as she held on to a sticky metal pole. *Note to self: wash my right hand ASAP.* A chorus line of cheap lilac perfume, stale pizza, and armpit BO took center stage, while hints of locker room and urine brought up the rear.

Most people had a weaker sense of smell than Jessica. *Sometimes, that must be a blessing. Like now*, she realized, glancing at the other passengers, all of whom appeared unaffected by the raunchy odor. She'd take barnyard smells over subway smells any day. She closed her eyes and focused on the lingering scent of juniper and citrus from her visit to Nick's office.

She gave in to daydreams of Nick. Or were they

memories from two years ago? Their monthlong relationship had been as hot and sticky as this train. The movement of the train intensified her fantasies. Thoughts of Nick pushed everything else out of her mind. The other passengers disappeared. The train vanished. Her dissertation and dreams of a PhD faded. There was only the rocking of their bodies, the scent of his hair, the softness of his lips . . . She sucked in a breath. The relationship was a mistake. The fantasies were a mistake. Swallowing the fetid air of the train car was a mistake.

Everything was a mistake.

When the train screeched to a stop at Melrose, so did her fantasies. She had to stop thinking about him. She'd spent two years trying to get over him. She thought she'd succeeded. That is, until tonight when everything came flooding back. *No, no, no.* A romantic relationship with Nick just wasn't in the cards. It was academically unethical, for crap's sake. And he was seven years older than her, and rich. He lived in another world. There were so many reasons she should just forget him and get on with her graduate career. She needed him on her committee, not in her bed.

She stepped out onto the platform. Nothing looked familiar. She glanced up at the sign to make sure she'd gotten off at the right stop. *Melrose.* It was her stop. She inhaled the street smells—urine, rot, and exhaust. She needed to clear her head. Hopefully, the fifteen-minute walk to her apartment would to do the trick.

Her phone buzzed. She slipped it from her pocket. Amber. *Finally!* Jessica had only left a dozen text messages in the last two hours. In her Nick-induced stupor, she'd almost forgotten she was on a mission to find Amber before the cops did.

"Amber! Where have you been?" She held the phone to her ear as she skipped down the stairs to the street. Even though it was just dusk, her girl-alone-at-night instincts kicked in. Her senses were on high alert.

"Gary and I were playing D&D with some friends in Skokie." Amber sounded as cheerful as always.

Dungeons and Dragons was some weird role-playing game nerds loved. Jessica preferred poker. It was good practice for life: do the math, and if the odds aren't in your favor, you'd better be damn good at bluffing. At least that's what she'd thought before she got to graduate school, where her life was one big bluff. *Imposter syndrome* was the technical term.

"I've got to see you," Jessica said, shifting her phone to her other ear as she scanned the street for creeps.

"What's up? Need a perm? Lash tint?" Before she'd returned to school, Amber had been a beautician. Her wacky ways and down-to-earth manner were a breath of fresh air after the stuffy Ivy League sorts strutting around Brentano Hall.

"Something happened tonight and I need to talk to you." Before turning onto her side street, Jessica glanced around. She'd feel better if more people were out and about. With her free hand, she dug her apartment key out of her pocket and maneuvered the jagged edge between her fingers to use as a weapon if necessary, then picked up her pace. Avoiding eye contact with passersby, she marched up the street toward her building. It was like this every night. The world was a dangerous place for a woman alone . . . maybe for anyone. *Just look at Nick's dad. All his money couldn't protect him.*

"Should I call Lolita and see if she wants to meet up at Pavlov's for shots?" Amber asked.

"I was hoping to talk to you alone." Jessica checked in every direction before she inserted her key into the lock of the door to her building. Her pulse raced as she twisted the key and slipped inside, shutting the door hard behind her.

Amber was whispering something to someone, probably Gary.

"Can't you ditch Gary and come alone?"

"I heard that," said a man's voice. She stopped in her tracks in front of her mailbox. *Crapulence!* Amber must have her on speakerphone.

More whispering. "Okay. Gary will drop me at Pavlov's and we can Uber back to Rogers Park together later."

"Great." Jessica smiled to herself. For a hippie chick, it was funny Amber refused to take public transportation. Usually she had her boyfriend chauffeur her around town. When Jessica first met Amber, that boyfriend had been Jack.

"See you in twenty." Jessica tapped her phone and wondered how she was going to get all the way to Skokie in twenty minutes. *Not using public transportation, that's for sure.*

Jessica would have preferred meeting someplace closer. Since they lived only three blocks from each other, it seemed kind of silly to meet in Skokie. *Oh well.* She called for a Lyft. At fifteen bucks, she'd have to skip Starbucks for the rest of the week.

PAVLOV'S BANQUET was an unassuming red brick building. Inside, it was like a Russian Disneyland, with flashing colored lights swirling around a postage-stamp dance floor. The walls were painted with nineteenth-century Moscow street scenes—a woman in an evening gown stepping out of a carriage; a couple walking arm-in-arm, both wearing fur coats and hats; a shop with windows full of pig carcasses and a fat butcher wearing a white apron smiling in the doorway. She cringed. The place wasn't exactly vegetarian friendly.

The tables wore baby-blue cloths, and the chairs were tied with giant red bows. The first time she'd brought Nick to Pavlov's, she'd joked that the tables were better dressed than she was. It was still true. She'd worn the fabric thin on most of her great-grandmother's vintage dresses, and her Wranglers had holes in them, but not the symmetrical fashionable kind.

Jessica glanced around the restaurant. *What the . . .* Amber was at the bar, throwing back a vodka shot. And next to her sat Lolita, whose long, silky black hair danced as she tossed back her frozen shot. So much for talking to Amber alone.

Good thing she trusted Lolita with her life. In fact, she'd owed her life to Lolita on more than one occasion. She chuckled to herself, remembering the time Lolita kicked those rapist frat boys' asses. In her black leather pants, and in spite of her fluffy pink midriff sweater, the Russian beauty was more feminist avenger than sex kitten. Men who confused the two sometimes regretted it. In what she wore and what she loathed, Lolita was predictable. What—or who—she loved was another story.

Amber, on the other hand, loved everyone, and you never knew what kind of weird hippie getup she'd have on. Tonight, her auburn curls sprung out in all directions from a purple paisley scarf tied around her head. Even under her baggy dress, you could make out her ample curves. And of course, she was wearing her ugly, beat-up UGGs. Jessica glanced down at her own boots, red model paint peeling off their toes. Maybe Amber wasn't the only one who needed some real shoes.

Amber spotted her and jumped up for a hug. "Lovey," she squealed, her voice raspy like she'd been yelling at a concert the night before. With her fleshy embrace came a cloud of patchouli that clung to Jessica as she claimed a barstool between her two friends.

"Hey Vanya," Lolita said to the bartender. They were second cousins. He'd started working at Pavlov's a couple months ago. "A frozen shot for my Montana friend." Lolita was a regular at Pavlov's. Her family practically owned the place.

"Going right up," Vanya said with a thick Russian accent. He'd recently been fired from his job as a security guard for punching out a racist cop. Hard to believe he was now slinging drinks. He'd never worked as a bartender before, as far as Jessica knew. Even with his wiry frame, a bouncer would be more believable. Pavlov's was well known as a viper's nest of Russian mobsters. Maybe Vanya was back working for the mob.

Jessica nodded when he brought her shot. She would have preferred a Jack & Coke, but she downed the shot before it could get warm and taste even worse. At least Lolita wasn't trying to make her eat *salo* along with it. Those disgusting slabs of pork fat were one of the only things she'd ever seen Lolita eat in public. Usually, her friend had a thing about eating in public. Jessica, on the other hand, ate everywhere: on the train, in class—she even sneaked food into the library. But she drew the line at blobs of raw fat or any other animal parts.

"Vanya, dearest," Lolita purred. "Can you bring us an order of *salo*?"

When Vanya smiled, the gold grill on his front teeth reflected the bar's low-hanging halogen lights.

"What's *salo*?" Amber asked.

"You don't want to know." Jessica shook her head.

Grinning like a goon, Vanya juggled three oranges, cut one into wedges, then refilled their shot glasses from a frozen bottle of Stoli. "Down the latch!" For a mobster, he was a hoot.

"Hatch," Jessica corrected.

"May we always have a reason to celebrate," Lolita said, raising her glass.

After clinking the chunky little vials of vodka, Jessica swallowed her shot in one gulp.

"So, what's with all the messages?" Amber twirled the straw in her frozen pink drink, which was crowned with a maraschino cherry and a tiny purple umbrella.

Jessica licked her finger and wiped something brown—hopefully chocolate—off Amber's forehead. "I thought you'd be alone."

"Can I help it if Lolita was already here?"

"Aren't you happy to see me, darling?" Lolita tossed her head back. "Where else would I be?"

"At a poker game . . . or at some country club scoping out marks for your next game," Jessica said. "They don't call you the Poker Tsarina for nothing." Lolita's high-stakes poker games attracted some of the deepest pockets in Chicago, and in spite of Detective Cormier's warnings, she'd continued hosting them. Not many people said no to Lolita.

Lolita laughed and slammed her glass down on the bar. "I'll stake you at the next game if you want to make your tuition in one night."

"I'm not that good." Jessica waved off the suggestion. "Anyway, I'm on a fellowship, so I don't pay any tuition."

"Smarty-pants." Amber took a piece of *salo* from the plate Vanya had placed in front of them. She examined it, licked it, and then took a teeny, tiny bite.

"I suppose fat is good for us now," Jessica said, waiting for her friend's reaction to the disgusting appetizer. Given Amber's obsession with herbal detox potions and green juice, she was surprised her friend would even try the slimy Russian delicacy.

"Fat is good for the brain," Amber said. "Except for animal fat—"

"What other kind of fat is there?" Lolita asked. Fat was something the Russian beauty didn't know anything about, not having an ounce of it on her tall, slim frame.

"I didn't come to talk about fat," Jessica said. She tapped her phone. "I came to talk about this." She showed Amber the picture she took of the tea bags.

"Hey, my homemade chamomile tea bags. They got their own photo shoot? Where's that?"

Jessica swiveled to face her friend. "The hotel room of a dead man." She handed her phone to Amber so she could look at the clandestine pictures from the crime scene. "What were your chamomile tea bags doing in Mr. Schilling's hotel room?" Amber wasn't as much of an airhead as she seemed, but she put on a good act.

Amber's face had gone as pale as the washed-out chamomile flowers in the photo. She hauled her Mary

Poppins purse onto her lap and started rummaging. She pulled out a tiny blue bottle, unscrewed the lid, and squeezed the dropper over her tongue. Amber, the Queen of Rescue Remedy.

Lolita took her turn looking at the pictures. "Who is Mr. Schilling?"

"Nick Schilling's dad."

Lolita's head whipped around so fast her jet hair lashed around her neck.

"Yeah, the very same." Jessica grabbed her phone. Lolita hadn't approved of her affair with Nick. And she'd been one of several.

"What do my tea bags have to do with Mr. Schilling?" Amber wiggled on her barstool. She never sat still.

"Hopefully, they don't have anything to do with Mr. Schilling's death." Jessica blew at her bangs. "But we've got to make sure the cops think the same.

Amber pinched the tiny rubber bulb and dropped more herbal tonic onto her tongue. She fumbled with her purse, looking for something else to rescue her.

"What's all this about?" Lolita motioned to Vanya for another round.

"Nick's dad was found dead in the penthouse of the Parker Hotel—"

"The Parker Penthouse," Lolita interrupted. "That's where I've been hosting my games since we got back from Vegas."

"The medical examiner thinks it's a heart attack,"

Jessica said. "But it just doesn't fit. I think he was poisoned. So does Detective Cormier."

"Poisoned?" Amber asked. She was tapping her head with one hand and her chest with the other, doing her weird energy-balancing thing. Jessica was used to it by now, although it was embarrassing when she started tapping Jessica's head in public. As a friend, she could only submit. Anyway, all the weird woo-woo crap meant Amber cared.

"There were two cups on a tea service." Jessica pointed at the bar. "That's where I took this picture." She turned to her friend. "Were you with Mr. Schilling earlier today?"

"You think I poisoned him!" Amber's face turned scarlet. "That's crazy."

"I'm not accusing you, but these are your tea bags. The cup had your signature shade of lipstick. And the room reeked of patchouli. I'm just trying to think like a cop."

"You've got an overactive imagination," Lolita scoffed. "Come on. Amber may be a computer wizard, but she couldn't plot herself out of a cardboard box." She reached out to touch Amber's arm. "No offense."

"Mr. Schilling is a VIP donor. I met him to get the pledge documents signed for work." Amber wrapped a snaky coil of hair around her finger and flipped the end into her mouth. "Anyway, lots of people wear patchouli. And purple lipstick."

"Uh, no they don't." Jessica shook her head. "I'm just

trying to help. Once the cops realize those are your tea bags, you'll be a prime suspect. And you're wearing the same purple lipstick now."

"I've given my tea bags to lots of people." Amber rubbed her hands together. "*You* have some."

"That's true." Jessica should never have pretended to like that nasty tea. She had a whole drawer full of them in her apartment. "Sorry, I sound like I'm interrogating you. I don't mean to. I'm just worried about you. We've got to clear this up before the cops come looking for you."

Lolita gestured toward the shots lined up on the bar. "Drink up, ladies. It's going to be an interesting night." She downed a shot. "Jessica, darling, do you have a pen?"

Of course she had a pen. She was an academic—more likely to leave her house without her wallet than a writing instrument. She produced said instrument from her beat-up book bag, which had already been a bit worn when she'd gotten it used at an Army-Navy surplus store. The military was good for some things.

Lolita held a bar napkin firmly with one hand and aimed the pen at it with the other. "Let's make a list of everyone you've made drink that dreg." She nodded toward the dried-up tea bags.

To the other patrons, the shriveled linen tea bags in the picture might have been some exotic desert insects the three women were studying for a school project.

"Gary likes it." Amber pouted.

"Gary," Lolita said as she wrote his name at the top of the napkin. "Who else?"

"Jessica has some." Amber reached over, grabbed the pen out of Lolita's hand, and scratched GARY off the list. "Come on, Gary wouldn't hurt a fly."

"After what happened to Nick's dad, I'm never touching that stuff again."

"Chamomile is relaxing, good for healing and sleeping—"

"Maybe it worked a little too well," Jessica interrupted. "Mr. Schilling is sleeping the sleep of the dead."

Lolita snatched her pen back and rewrote GARY in big letters.

Amber scowled and then named a few other friends and coworkers. Lolita added their names to the list. They were up to eight.

"Did you give any to Nick?" Jessica asked, trying to sound nonchalant. Nick had the most to gain from his father's death.

"I haven't seen Nick since you two were—"

"How about someone he works with at the center?" Jessica didn't want to talk about her affair with Nick. "That horrible Sally woman or Lolita's dad?"

Lolita frowned. "What does Dad have to do with this? Why does everyone always suspect the Russians?"

"I'm just asking because I saw your dad at Nick's Center for Russian Art and Culture and—"

"He works there now as a curator. No more cleaning other people's shit for a living." Lolita picked at the paint on one of her fingernails. "I know he was trying to lay low, but two decades as a janitor? Really?"

"I didn't think anything embarrassed you—" Jessica said.

"I wasn't embarrassed, just humiliated for him."

"Really? That humiliated you, but you weren't humiliated your grandfather was one of the biggest mob bosses in the world." Jessica's face grew hot. "What about the fact that your dad was mixed up in the Russian mafia art scam? That's not humiliating?"

"Better than cleaning toilets."

"Better in what sense?" Jessica had grown up in a trailer park. She resented her friend looking down her nose at working-class folks.

"I'm not going to debate philosophy with you." Lolita twisted her hair into a bun, securing it with the pen.

Jessica realized she'd gotten distracted. She was supposed to be helping Amber clear her name. Why were they talking about humiliation? "Amber, you still haven't explained why you were having tea with Mr. Schilling."

"I told you, he is—was—a donor. He seemed nervous. I thought the tea would calm him down."

Jessica's phone vibrated and skittered across the bar. She glanced down at the screen. *What the chuck?* A text message from her dissertation director. Never a good sign. Two years had gone by and Jessica still hadn't turned in the last chapter of her dissertation. And she'd been avoiding her advisor for the last three months. With trepidation, she opened it.

"Holy shit . . ." Her voice trailed off.

"What's wrong?" Lolita asked. When Jessica didn't answer, she snatched the phone and read the message for herself.

"Whoa. They're putting you on probation?"

"So it seems." The philosophy department had given her until the end of the fall semester to finish her dissertation, or get kicked out of the program.

"That's not fair," Lolita said, putting her hands on her hips. "Have they put any dudes on probation?"

"Nope." None of the dudes were ever put on probation. As usual, she had to do to better than any man to reap the same rewards. She'd learned that lesson long ago, back home in Montana as a rodeo rider.

She did the math in her head, figuring out how many pages she'd have to write each day from now until the middle of December. If she wrote a page a day, she might make it. In her mind's eye, she watched her dream of becoming a college professor die a slow, painful death. Maybe her mom was right and she'd be better off slinging hash in some Whitefish dive and coming home to a husband, two brats, a few horses, and a dog. If she didn't get her butt in gear, she could end up like her mother, a fifth of vodka in one hand and a bottle of Xanax in the other.

6

The Toyota minivan's tires squealed as Dmitry rounded the corner. He skidded to a stop in his driveway. His pulse quickened as he strode up the sidewalk past his wife's precious rosebushes toward the house. *Why is the house dark? Where is she?*

"Blyad!" he said under his breath. He'd been in the United States long enough now that even his dreams were in English, but when he was enraged, the curse words always burst out in Russian.

Hands shaking, he fumbled with his house key, turned the doorknob, and silently slipped inside. His breath caught when he heard voices coming from the back. Sabina wasn't alone.

He crept through the living room toward the back of the house. They'd been here only a year, and he still wasn't used to having so much space. The small three-bedroom, two-story house was twice as big as their last place. Granted, the last house was only a thousand square feet and felt crowded with just the three of them and Bunin, their German shepherd.

Without turning on the lights, he made his way through the living room and down the hallway to the kitchen. He stopped just short of the entrance and listened. *Suka blyad. How in the hell did he get here before me?* He inhaled deeply and stepped into the room.

Like the rest of the house, the kitchen was decorated with Sabina's touch. She'd sewn bright floral curtains for the windows and had him hang special hooks for her favorite copper frying pans. She'd been thrilled to have more counter space and a dishwasher. He gazed at his wife. From her diminutive stature and girlish good looks, you'd never know she was damaged but not broken.

Sabina was serving tea from the samovar. Her movements were ghostly, as if her body were on autopilot while her mind was elsewhere. She hadn't been the same since the fire that had burned their little house in Skokie and almost killed her. If it hadn't been for Bunin, she'd be dead.

"Dima," she said. "Look who's risen from the dead." Her hands trembled as she handed Sergei a cup of tea. When her eyes met Dmitry's, he saw terror and a silent plea for help. He wanted more than anything to protect her—that's all he'd ever wanted, to protect those he loved.

"No thanks to my dear brother, who left me for dead twenty years ago," Sergei said with a smirk.

"At least I didn't kill you." Dmitry took a seat at the table. He'd been only nineteen, for God's sake. No wonder he'd left Moscow.

He nodded to his wife when she handed him a cup of tea. He took one sip, then another. The strong tea would help fortify him against whatever might come next. He glanced at his brother. As a boy, he had tortured animals. As a grown man, he was capable of anything.

"That was your first mistake." Sergei grinned. "Stealing my inheritance was your last."

"All the money I took was burned in a fire." Dmitry extended his open palms. Unfortunately, it was true. When Vanya burned their house down two years ago, all the money he'd been hiding over two decades went up in smoke. He should have spent it instead of hiding it, but, like the past, he was afraid of it. Like the past, it felt better just to bury it. "It was hidden under the floorboards when the house burned to the ground. The dog pulled Sabina through his doggie door, or she'd be dead." He shuddered just saying the words out loud. He glanced over at his wife, whose soft brown eyes had hardened into sharp rocks.

"There are worse things than death," Sergei said. He wasn't smiling anymore.

"The same hammer that breaks glass forges steel," Dmitry said in Russian. He remembered his mother telling him that when he was eighteen and his father made him drop out of art school to join the "family business." The question was had standing up to his father and leaving home broken him or strengthened him?

His shirt was damp with sweat, and the tea was just making him hotter. He had to get Sergei out of his house and out of his life. He should have killed him when he had the chance. *If I had, I'd still be in Moscow. Hell, maybe I'd be the head of Bratva.* He shook his head. That's exactly what he left to escape. He was an artist, not a thug.

"Sabina, would you excuse us?" When Sergei reached across the table and patted her hand, she flinched. "Dima and I have business to discuss."

Sabina refused to make eye contact as she stood up and left the room. She hated Sergei more than Dmitry did. Maybe she hated his brother for giving her what she loved most. Dmitry pushed those painful thoughts from his mind. He wanted nothing more than to rush after her and wrap her in his arms. He'd escaped Russia and his father in order to keep her safe. But in truth, she was his safe haven, his refuge from the violence of the world.

"Okay, Sergei. Quit playing games. What in the hell do you want?" Dmitry clenched his fists. He may kill his brother yet.

Even Sabina's strong black tea wasn't enough to fortify Dmitry against the nightmare of Sergei's resurrection. The tip missing from Sergei's left ear took him back to a grisly scene from his adolescence. His father had sent him and his brother on an "errand." They were to collect protection money from a knife-wielding shop owner who was tired of paying Bratva just to stay in business. Blood spurting from his ear, Sergei had kicked the knife out of the shop owner's hand and gutted the guy.

"Sabina's looking as beautiful as ever," Sergei grinned. "Stealing my girl was your second mistake."

Dmitry shot his brother a dirty look, then dragged himself up from the table. His limbs were heavy, and it took all his effort. Seeing Sergei had sucked the life out of him. He thought of his mother. Leaving her had been the hardest thing he'd ever done. And it was Sergei's fault for being such a stupid, greedy *mudak*, thinking he could embezzle from Bratva and get away with it. *What did he expect?*

Dmitry took a bottle of Stoli from the freezer. Lolita kept it there for her weekly visits. *Is drinking the only way she can deal with us?* He loved his daughter dearly, but she was a mystery. She didn't share her thoughts, dreams, or plans. She was so secretive. Maybe she came by it naturally. He, too, had his secrets. Being a foreigner wasn't easy. Being the son of the most infamous organized crime boss in the world meant keeping secrets or facing death. Still, in the end, no matter how faithful you were to your secrets, no one could escape death.

"Ah, good idea," Sergei said in Russian. "Tea is for sissies."

Dmitry held the bottle in one hand and grabbed two shot glasses with the other. The glasses clinked as he walked back to the table. Again, he thought of his mother's favorite saying. *The same hammer that breaks glass forges steel.* Could his fear of his brother be that hammer? Whatever Sergei wanted, he wasn't going to get it. He set the glasses on the table and poured out two shots.

Sergei grabbed his, threw it back, then slammed his glass on the table. He snatched the bottle from Dmitry's hand and poured himself another. He gulped it down and poured another. His nostrils flared, skin glistening like polished leather.

Dmitry was tempted to match him drink for drink. But he knew that wouldn't end well. "So, *moy brat*, what do you want?" He held the Russian for *my brother* between his teeth like a dirty rag.

"I want what you stole. As the older son, it's rightfully mine."

As the only son. The last time he saw her, Dmitry's mother had confessed that Anton Yudkovich—also known as "the Oxford Don"—was not his father. "I told you, the rubles burned in a house fire set by one of the goons the Pope sent to threaten me. I don't take well to threats." Dmitry imagined seizing the vodka bottle, smashing it against the table, and using a shard of glass as a weapon. He didn't mention that the goon was his cousin Vanya or that the Pope was after the Kandinsky paintings.

"I know you took art too. I heard about the paintings. Too bad about your professor friend." Sergei poured another shot.

"He wasn't my friend." The late Professor Schmutzig had been blackmailing him, and, as much as he abhorred violence, Dmitry had to admit he wasn't sorry to see the smug professor poisoned by one of his own students.

"Too bad," Sergei repeated, clucking his tongue. "Accidents happen if we aren't careful. Dead professors, house fires . . . sounds like you are accident-prone, dear brother."

"I don't have any money. What do you want from me?" Dmitry rubbed his forehead.

"Oh, but I know you do. I know you recently sold those ridiculous paint splotches for a tidy little fortune. I want my share. It's only fair, don't you think?" Sergei stroked his neatly trimmed mustache.

"Look, Sergei. I told you, I don't have any money." Dmitry's palms were sweating. "My house burned down. I didn't have insurance; I had to sell the paintings to buy a new house."

Sergei shook his head.

"I didn't want to sell them. I loved them like my children." That wasn't quite true. He'd loved the Kandinsky, but the Goncharova—his mother's favorite piece—had always irritated him. Goncharova's blocky, primitive, figures seemed crude compared to Kandinsky's elegant lines.

"You're going to give me my share one way or another, brother." Sergei patted his pocket. "One way or another."

"I sold the paintings to Mr. Nick. They're hanging in his new museum, the Center for Russian Art and Culture. I spent all the money already. This house—Lolita's tuition . . ." Sergei didn't deserve the truth. Dmitry had sold the Goncharova to buy his new house. But he'd never sell the Kandinsky. It was on loan. He couldn't bear to part with it, not ever. That painting had gotten him through many a dark night. Anyway, he didn't owe Sergei a single ruble. If anything, his brother owed Dmitry his life back. All he'd ever wanted was a regular life, nothing special—working, painting, loving his wife and daughter. He didn't want wealth or fame or power. He just wanted to be left in peace. "I'm sorry, Sergei. I don't have anything to give you."

"But you do, Dimka. You do."

Dmitry shuddered at the familiarity of his childhood nickname. "Just tell me what you want and then leave my house."

"I have a buyer for three Kandinsky paintings. A ridiculous banker in Moscow needs them to fill out his collection. They're in your museum. He's willing to pay serious rubles. You get them for me and you'll never see me again."

"I can't." Dmitry tugged at his collar. "They belong

to the Center. I don't own them." Technically, he never had, since he'd stolen them from his father. Actually, that wasn't quite true either—his mother had given them to him as a parting gift. Thoughts of her conjured the scent of rose water and took Dmitry back to the train platform where he'd said goodbye to her all those years ago.

"You work there. Go get them back." Sergei raised his voice.

"What? Steal paintings from the museum? Are you crazy?" He clenched his fists.

"I told my buyer I'd have them for him by the end of the month. You've got two weeks to get them for me, or else—" A vein popped out in his neck.

"Or else what? You're going to pull my hair or kick me like you did when we were kids?" He glared at his brother.

"Speaking of kids," Sergei lowered his voice. "Your lovely daughter is going to host a game for me." He grinned. "Lolita," he whispered. "The lovely Lolita."

Dmitry lunged across the table. Both glasses went flying and shattered against the tile floor. *The same hammer . . .* His fingers grazed Sergei's lapel as his brother jumped up from his chair.

"Sit down!" Sergei snatched up the vodka bottle before it could topple. He sat it on the table, then brushed droplets from his jacket. "Sit down." He whispered this time. "There's no need for violence . . . " His voice trailed off. He might as well have added "not yet."

He pulled his chair out, sat back down, then pointed at Dmitry's chair. "Sit!"

Like a well-trained dog, Dmitry obeyed.

"Enough with the pleasantries, brother," Sergei said, running his fingers through his graying hair. "You've been lying to me and I know it."

Dmitry slumped in his chair. Why would he think anything had changed? He never could fight Sergei and win.

"Yes. You sold mother's favorite painting to Nick Schilling. But you didn't sell your beloved, and much more valuable, Kandinsky. You loaned it to your precious Center." Sergei grinned.

"I signed an agreement. I can't take it back."

"Oh, yes you can, and you will. I have a plan to get that painting and more, plus my money—the money you stole from father."

"I didn't steal it." Dmitry met his brother's beady stare. "Mother gave it to me."

"*Mother gave it to me,*" Sergei repeated in a mocking voice. "You're pathetic."

"What's your plan?" *Might as well get this over with.*

Sergei put his hand inside his jacket pocket, removed an MSS VUL silent pistol, and sat it on the table. Then he took out a folded sheet of paper.

Dmitry reached for the gun.

"No you don't." Sergei snatched up the pistol. He weighed the gun in his hand and then laughed. "Remember the last time you held this pistol?"

Unfortunately, as hard as Dmitry tried, he couldn't forget it. The clatter of the VUL hitting the concrete floor had echoed through the abandoned hospital. Even now, that sound haunted him. He shuddered.

"You couldn't do it, could you?" Sergei pocketed the gun. "You're still as weak as ever." He unfolded the paper and used his palms to flatten it on the table. "Here, brother, is the plan." He slid the paper to Dmitry. "Do this one thing and I'll vanish from your life forever."

7

Amber Bush was in over her curly head. She'd stayed out too late at Pavlov's the night before and morning had come way too early. She'd woken up at dawn, worrying about wayward tea bags and Jessica's suspicions . A couple drops of Rescue Remedy and a nice cup of chamomile tea would calm her down. She sniffed the dry tea bag, the same blend she'd given Mr. Schilling. *And now he's dead.*

She put the kettle on and removed a cup from the dish rack as quietly as she could so as not to wake Gary. She wished she'd gone home instead of coming back to Gary's. Even after two years together, she always felt like an intruder rummaging around his apartment before he got up. She dropped the tea bag into the cup and grabbed a loaf of gluten-free bread from the freezer to make a piece of toast.

Gary's kitchen reminded her of a mad scientist's

laboratory, with gadgets and test tubes. Instead of glasses, Gary drank out of beakers. The warped linoleum, cracked Formica counter, and stained sink made the kitchen feel dingy no matter how much she scrubbed.

"Sweetie, come back to bed," Gary called from the other room. "It's not even daylight."

"I'm making some tea," she called back. "Want some?" She put the kettle on the stove and turned the burner on high. The familiar clicking of the gas igniting reassured her. She stood frozen, hypnotized by the flickering blue flame, with her hand resting on the kettle's handle.

A rustling from the bedroom made her turn around. Wearing only his boxers, Gary ambled into the kitchen. He yawned as he put his arms around her waist and then rested his head on her shoulder.

"Why are you up?" he whispered into her neck. "Come back to bed." His touch was gentle and loving.

She poured boiling water into two cups and handed one to Gary. "Morning Thunder blend," she said with a smile.

"Why can't we just have coffee in the morning like normal people?" Gary grumbled.

"Coffee is bad for you . . . unless you take it as an enema."

"Wrong end, Sweetie. Forget I mentioned it." He took a sip of tea, then made a sour face.

"Remember when you said we'd be better off

without the 1 percent?" She twirled a coil of hair around her finger.

"Where did that come from?" He chuckled. "It's too early to talk politics. I never talk politics before my first cup of coffee." He sat his teacup on the kitchen counter, went to the cupboard and pulled out a can of coffee. "But in a word, yes. Working-class folks like my dad die in coal mines while the owners prosper." He scooped fresh, black grounds into the Mister Coffee maker. "There won't be justice until we have a redistribution of wealth."

"A redistribution. Maybe that's what someone was doing by killing one of the donors." She sipped her tea. Ever since Gary had joined the Young Socialists on campus, he'd become so serious. She wasn't sure she really knew him anymore. "One of the VIPER donors died." She was afraid to tell him about her tea bags. He'd see her meeting with Mr. Schilling as a betrayal.

"VIPER?" he asked as he filled the machine with water.

"*VIPER* stands for VIP Estate Retirement, where 'retirement' really means 'death.' He was a donor to that new Center for Russian Art. Some rich guy Jessica knew."

"One less rich guy. So what?" He flipped the switch and the coffee machine gurgled to life.

"He'd just signed a VIPER plan."

"No doubt a tax write-off."

"Weird he dies the day after he signs the document leaving his art collection and two million dollars to the Center."

"*So-called* donation. It's a scam to keep his heirs from paying estate tax." Gary poured himself a cup of strong coffee. "He probably donated because he was at death's door. So it's not that weird he died."

"But the very next day?" She sipped her tea.

Gary topped off his cup with cream and then took a sip. "That's more like it!" he sighed.

Amber put the kettle back on to boil. When she'd first met Gary two years ago, he'd been a biology nerd in love with poison dart frogs and online chess. Now his politics scared her. Not that she didn't agree with him in theory . . . but sometimes he went too far.

"Wow, what an idea." Gary laughed. "The university gets rich bastards to sign over their estates when they die and then offs them."

She narrowed her brows. "That's not nice. A man just died."

"Sorry." He buried his hands in his mop of brown hair. "Why do you care so much about some rich dude?"

"Jessica found my chamomile tea bags in his room."

"What? Why?"

"She says I'm a suspect now." Amber's lip trembled. She wished she hadn't tampered with the document. *What if the cops find out? Will I go to jail?*

"You? Kill someone?" He snickered. "Maybe by accident with your horrible herbal remedies."

The dig hurt, but she wasn't going to be distracted. She took a deep breath. *Here goes!* "It was Richard Schilling." She crinkled her nose.

Gary stiffened. "Julie," he whispered.

"Yeah, Julie," Amber repeated. She shook her head, not wanting to think about Gary's poor sister. What Mr. Schilling had done to her. Instead, she focused on the meeting. "And Schilling had Lila with him the first time I met with him."

"Lila? From Girls First ?" He narrowed his eyes. "The scumbag deserved to die. Exploiting refugee girls . . . Deviant bastard." He slammed his coffee cup onto the counter.

"Yesterday, Amira was with him. She wasn't feeling well, so I gave her some of my special Tummy Blend. He had some too." Amber wrapped a curl around her finger and resisted the temptation to slip it into her mouth. Now she felt sick. Maybe she should have said something to the director of Girls First about Lila and Amira. They were only teenagers. *What were they doing with a grown man?* But Mr. Schilling said he was helping the girls. He gave them money to help them, not to hurt them.

"Amira?" Gary scowled. "The girl who refuses to speak? I wish I'd killed the bastard. Trafficking refugee girls . . . What's wrong with these filthy rich men?"

"Mr. Schilling said he was helping her—"

"Don't be so naive." Gary shook his head. "Maybe Amira killed him. It would serve him right."

"She's only seventeen." Was Amira capable of murder? "Yesterday, when we met, Mr. Schilling seemed anxious." Amber sighed. "I think he was waiting for his wife."

"Well, there's your murderer." Gary said. "After all, poison is the weapon of choice for jealous wives." He sat his cup on the counter. "If you're not coming back to bed, I'd best get dressed and go to the lab."

Amber reached into the pocket of her robe and pulled out the vial of Rescue Remedy. She dropped more of the bitter liquid under her tongue and waited for it to take effect. She needed something to calm her down.

"My frogs need feeding." Gary disappeared into the bedroom. He never went into the lab this early. "Do you have any extra manila envelopes?"

She pursed her lips. "What?"

"You're always carrying around those big envelopes." He emerged wearing khaki pants and an oxford shirt. "You had a stack of them here last week."

She narrowed her eyes. "Those are for work. Why?"

"Never mind."

She wrapped a coil of hair around her finger and popped the end into her mouth. She still couldn't believe it. She'd had tea with Mr. Schilling just yesterday afternoon and now he was dead. He'd promised to sign the pledge documents and mail them back. Amber wondered whether he had before he died. Did the tea bags really make her a suspect? Was Amira a suspect, too? Did the police even know she'd been there? *It's going to be okay*, she told herself. *Everything happens for a reason*.

8

Nick sat at his desk, staring at a white envelope. It looked exactly like the one Detective Cormier had shown him the previous day, in his father's hotel room. The envelope had just arrived in the post from the University Development Office. He turned it over, opened it with his Swiss Army knife, and withdrew the contents— a copy of his father's donation agreement with the Center.

Nick thumbed through the documents. They were stamped UNSIGNED COPY. Maybe his father's death meant the donation was no longer valid . . . then again, he'd already signed the other documents before he died. An accompanying letter from the Development Office indicated the signed copies would be coming soon.

A paragraph on page eight caught his eye. He pulled it closer and started reading in earnest. *What the—?*

The document stipulated that the Center would receive his father's art collection, but every month, it would sell one painting and split the proceeds. So *this* was what that "business associate" had been talking about. His father had been planning to use the Center to launder money. *Figures.* Now the sudden interest in philanthropy made sense. And Nick had thought the two paintings he'd already sold for his dad might be the end of it. *Fat chance.*

What about the two million dollars? Was that some shady tax write-off or money-laundering scheme, too? That donation would give the Center legs. He continued reading the document, which was mostly legalese. But it promised the two million dollars and the entire Russian art collection, along with some jewelry. He skipped to the end to see the bit about Russian refugees the detective had mentioned. He couldn't find it. He started over at the beginning, running his finger down each page. Nothing. He scanned each page again. Nope. This copy didn't contain the refugee provision. *Weird.* Why would his selfish, money-grubbing dad leave money to refugees? He must have had a change of heart.

The phone rang and he answered it. *Shit.* It was a member of the museum board. What did he want?

"I heard you raised enough money to hire permanent staff," Bob Marshall said in a demanding tone.

This guy didn't beat around the bush. "Actually, yes, we may have a big donation coming in soon." *But how could he have heard about it? Dad* just *signed the paperwork.*

"Now you'll be able to promote Sally to the assistant director position."

"Actually, I already have an offer out to a stellar young scholar just finishing her PhD." Nick wrote *Jessica* on the envelope and drew a little heart next to it.

"I thought you were going to promote Sally."

It figured. Trustees and board members would be pressuring him to hire their children and second-cousins and who knew what else. Just because Bob Marshall had donated to the Center didn't give him the right to make demands. Sally was doing a fine job as an intern, but she didn't have Jessica's keen intelligence . . . and there was just something about the perfect little rich girl that set Nick's teeth on edge.

"My daughter, Sally Marshall. She's graduating from college this year and majoring in art—against my wishes, too, I might add."

Nick was tempted to quote the many studies demonstrating the financial benefits of *any* humanities degree, but he thought better of it. "Sally. She's doing a great job as an intern." *Instead of donating tens of thousands to the museum and the university, why didn't daddy just hire his beloved daughter himself?* "I'm sure she'll find the perfect job."

"Sally is bright and responsible. She'll be a great assistant director."

"I'll consider Sally if the other candidate rejects my

offer." He leaned back in his chair. *Jesus*. His father had used the museum to sell paintings and launder money—then turned up dead in a hotel room. Now a trustee expected him to promote his daughter. What the hell would be next?

The sound of high heels on the tile interrupted his meditations. He glanced up and saw his father's widow standing in the doorway. *Shit. What is she doing here?* From the moment he'd met her, Nick could tell Chrissy Schilling was one of those women who'd learned from an early age that beauty was a powerful weapon if you knew how to wield it. And she did. Chrissy leaned against the doorframe, weeping into a floral handkerchief.

"Nicky. Isn't it awful?" She bit her lip.

"What are you doing here?" he asked, unable to conceal his annoyance. Were those tears real or an act? Did she really expect him to go over and comfort her?

"I came as soon as I heard." She sniffed. "Poor Richard."

She must have caught the first flight from New York . . . or Paris, or wherever she'd been. His father hadn't been dead twenty-four hours.

"His heart gave out, I'm afraid." He tried not to think of poison. Although if anyone was capable of killing his father, it was Chrissy.

Rivulets of mascara trickled down her cheeks. Nick couldn't take it anymore. He got up from his desk and went over to her. Maybe her distress was real. Was she actually distraught about "poor Richard"? Or was it his money she'd miss?

"Oh, Nicky," she said as she fell into his arms.

Her musky Shalimar perfume reminded Nick of his mother. His father gave it to all his wives. Nick closed his eyes. He hadn't seen his mother since she started shooting her latest film in Egypt, months ago. They used to talk on the phone every week. But since she'd become a movie star, her calls were less frequent and she wasn't always easy to reach.

"What will I do now?" Chrissy whined. "Will you take care of me? Promise you'll take care of me."

"You'll be fine." Nick pried her fingers off his neck. "You just need time to mourn, and so do I."

"At least we have each other," she said, gazing up at him with her soft amber eyes.

Although her cheeks were wet, her eyes weren't swollen or red from crying. *Is she manipulating me?* Perhaps his mother wasn't the only actress.

"You can throw yourself into your work. That's what I plan to do." Nick turned to go back to his desk. He'd had enough of her waterworks display.

"Yes, your precious Center." She threw her head back and shook out her hair. "It's a shame Richard died before he signed off on the donation." She smoothed her skirt.

"But he didn't." Nick smiled. He'd seen the signed documents in his father's hotel suite. Detective Cormier had showed them to him. He was sure they had been signed.

"What do you mean?" She sauntered across the office and perched on the edge of a leather chair.

"He signed everything before he died." He sat back down and folded his hands in his lap. "All the paperwork for the donation is complete."

"Impossible!" Her lips quivered.

"It's true." *Did she think she was inheriting everything?*

"Promise you won't let them put me out on the street," she simpered.

"I'm sure you won't be out on the street." He shook his head.

"You mean I get the house?" Her voice perked up.

"I don't know anything about Dad's will. I'm sure he left you something." He couldn't believe she was thinking about the will the day after his father's death. Actually, he could believe, all too well. What was wrong with this woman? He shuffled through the papers on this desk.

"I gave him my prime years." She sniffed. "He was already an old man. And I gave him my best years. I deserve something."

She deserved a kick to her skinny ass. "I really have to get back to work." He pointed at the stack of papers on his desk.

"Will you come to my hotel for a drink later?" She bit her lip again.

"I don't know if that's a good—"

"Please, Nicky. I don't want to be alone," she pleaded.

He shook his head and sighed. The conniving little witch had been playing him ever since she married his father. Even at the wedding, she'd come on to him. No way he was going to meet her in her hotel room.

She collapsed into the chair and sobbed.

She was making so much noise even the security guard down in his booth would hear her. Nick closed his office door.

"I don't want to go on living." Her shoulders heaved. "I've lost my job. I've lost my husband. I don't have anything else to live for."

He stood next to her chair and patted her on the shoulder.

"Please come to my hotel tonight. It's important. I have to show you something. Please, Nicky. Just for a few minutes—" She blew her nose into a tissue. Her tears were real. Maybe she did love his dad.

"Okay, okay. Stop crying." He retrieved the Waterford pen from his pocket and held it over a notepad. "What hotel?"

"Parker. Room 817." She dabbed at her eyes. "Come by at seven." She stood up, straightened her tight-fitting dress, and sauntered out of the office. "Don't forget," she said, turning back to flash her million-dollar smile.

"I won't." He shook his head.

The last thing he needed was more time with his father's conniving wife. He really did have work to do.

The grand opening of the Center was only a week away. And he still had to persuade Jessica to join the team. She was perfect for the job—brilliant, creative, high-energy but down-to-earth. And he had to admit, he would love having her around.

He thought about the night they'd met, at Lolita's poker game. There was something endearing about the way she'd kept tripping over those ridiculous high heels . . . and the sweet smell of her little black dress covered in Starbucks Frappuccino had sent his head spinning. The wilderness in her heart made him want to follow her into untamed forests and forget about the rest of the world.

He took his phone from his jeans' pocket and hit "Dolce" on speed dial.

"Nick, how are you doing?"

Her melodious voice was soothing. He could listen to it for the rest of his life.

"I'm okay all things considered." Actually, given the circumstances, he was doing pretty good . . . too good? He should be feeling something—pain, grief, anger, anything. But he felt hollow. *What's wrong with me?*

"Are you sure? You sound strange."

"It's been a strange day." He shifted the phone from one hand to the other.

"How so?"

"I'll tell you over dinner tonight." Before she could object, he added, "It won't be a long dinner. I'm meeting Chrissy at seven."

"Chrissy?"

"My father's wife. Widow." He twisted his class ring around his little finger.

"She's here?"

"She flew in as soon as she heard the news."

"Are you sure she wasn't here all along?" Jessica asked with a wry tone.

"You mean before dad's death?" He sat up straight.

"That would be convenient if she wanted to kill him."

"He died of a heart attack. Anyway, why would she want to kill him?"

"Greed. Why else? And I still say he was poisoned."

"I'm sure he had a prenup." He leaned his elbows on the desk. "He always did. He was worth more to her alive." He'd have to ask Mr. Randall, his father's lawyer.

"How can you be sure?"

Was Jessica cross-examining him? She'd make a good lawyer.

"How about we discuss Chrissy's scheming over dinner tonight. Can I pick you up at six?"

"I don't know. I only have a couple of months to finish this last chapter of my dissertation." She sighed. "I have writer's block. I'm totally stuck."

"All the more reason to join me for dinner. We can talk about your project. Maybe talking about it will help."

"Maybe."

"I know it will. Talking about my work always helps

me." It was true. And his conversations with Jessica were some of the most inspiring.

"Okay. You know where to find me. My regular table at Blind Faith."

He hung up, considerably cheered by the prospect of seeing sweet Jessica in just a few hours. Now to get some work done.

Sally Marshall appeared in the doorway. "Who were you talking to? That person you want to hire for the assistant director job?"

How long was she standing there? And what right does she have to ask me who I'm talking to? "Yes, Jessica James. I hope she accepts the position."

Sally scoffed, turned on her heels, and said—under her breath but just loud enough to hear—"I hope she drops dead."

9

Jessica was sitting at her usual booth in the back corner of Blind Faith Café. Worrying about her dissertation and Amber's teabags, she hadn't slept since they'd found Mr. Schilling's body. Her head hurt, and her eyes felt like they were drooling down her face. The familiar smells of spicy herbal teas and cakes buoyed her. Under the dim lights, her computer screen glowed while her blinking cursor lulled her to sleep. She lightly slapped her cheeks to try to wake up. She had to write something, but the words wouldn't come.

The department had given her an ultimatum: finish her dissertation or get kicked out of the program. If she couldn't write the damned thing in the next two months, her grad career would be down the drain with nothing to show for it. She could hear her mother's voice saying, "I told you so. You should have stayed home and married Bill Silverton when he asked you at high school graduation. If you had, you'd be the mayor's wife and I'd be a grandma."

Screw that! Whitefish, Montana, was the last place she wanted to end up. Sure, it was beautiful . . . beautiful but deadly boring. She flinched at the thought of living next door to her mom in a double-wide with a couple of snot-nosed kids. No thanks. She'd take her chances with the stuck-up jerks in the philosophy department.

And what about Amber? That hair-chewing was a sure giveaway. *What is she hiding?* Those were her tea bags and her lipstick. She was in that hotel room. Jessica was determined to find out what was going on. If she didn't, her friend could end up in prison on a murder rap.

Sigh. Jessica was exhausted. She couldn't think straight. No way Amber could be involved in a murder. She put her head in her hands. *One thing at a time.* Right now, she had to concentrate on her dissertation and get something written before Nick picked her up for dinner. Nick might have some new information about the investigation. She would worry about Amber later. Now, she had to write.

Maybe some banana nut pancakes would inspire her. Or should she save up her appetite for dinner? *Nah.* She had enough appetite to go around. She ordered a stack with extra whipped cream and a fresh pot of

Witch's Brew tea. After all, dinner wasn't for another six hours.

While she waited for her pancakes, she went online and checked her e-mail. The ultimatum message from her advisor was still there. She shouldn't look at it, but she opened it and stared. *Salt in the wound.* She closed her e-mail and googled The Russian Center for Art and Culture. Nick's picture popped up on the homepage. That luscious bottom lip, those thick arched brows and wavy chestnut hair. Her heart skipped a beat. He was too beautiful.

She scrolled through the pictures and imagined working there in that swanky building . . . with him. If she took the job, maybe she wouldn't have to finish the stupid dissertation. And if she dropped out and didn't finish her dissertation, then she could go out with Nick. Apart from the fact dropping out now would be like taking a wrecking ball to her self-esteem, it seemed worth considering. But no way would she give her mother the satisfaction. She was going to finish the damned dissertation and get her degree if it killed her.

But first, just one more look. She studied Nick's picture. He was only thirty and he'd already done so much with his life. He'd gotten tenure at a major university, he'd founded the Center, and he'd put together one of the most impressive Russian art collections in the country. Of course, unlike Jessica, he hadn't started his life in a trailer park in the backwoods of Montana. She thought of her mom drinking away the pain of her dead-end life. She chuckled to herself. If her mom thought Bill Silverton was a catch, what would she think of Nick?

She still couldn't face the blank screen, so next she googled Richard Schilling to see if there was any more news about his death. The *Chicago Tribune* reported the sixty-seven-year-old New York real estate and casino mogul died of an apparent heart attack in the penthouse suite of the Parker Hotel. He'd just signed a major estate donation to his son's new Center for Russian Art and Culture. By coincidence, no sooner was the ink dry on the donation than he keeled over. Well, that was the gist of it, anyway. *Convenient coincidence for the Center*, Jessica thought.

Her phone buzzed. It was Nick again.

"Dolce, can I pick you up now?" His voice cracked. "Detective Cormier wants to question me and I want you along."

"I doubt the detective will allow me in the room."

"You have a history with him."

"Right. That's why I say he won't let me in."

"I really don't want to go alone. It would help me so much if you went along for moral support. I'd be eternally grateful."

How could she refuse? "Why not? My writing is stalled anyway." She still had two months. She could finish the last chapter on time if she buckled down—even if she took a break now. She remembered her pancakes. "This is the second time in as many days you've made me miss my banana nut pancakes."

"I promise I'll make it up to you with extra syrup," he said playfully.

"That's a tall order. I *love* those pancakes." A memory of Nick in his robe making her breakfast flashed into her head.

"I hope I'm up to the challenge." The sound of his laughter brought back more memories of their glorious month together. She gritted her teeth. What was she getting into?

"Me too," she said and hung up.

The dog-collared waitress was just delivering her pancakes when Nick showed up at her table. Jessica asked for a to-go box, and Nick picked up the check.

"It's the least I can do," he said when she objected.

She tugged on her jacket, slung her backpack over her shoulder, grabbed the to-go box, and followed Nick outside to his fancy car.

Once they were on the road, Nick took her hand in his. "Thank you, Dolce. I really appreciate this."

She nodded. The warmth of his hand sent sparks up her arm. They rode the rest of the way to the station in silence, except for the beating of her heart, which was pounding so hard she was sure he could hear it too.

Nick circled around the Chicago Central Police Station, looking for a place to park. As he pulled into an expensive pay lot a couple of blocks away, the sky opened up with a clap of thunder. Nick dashed around to the passenger's side with an umbrella, and Jessica took his arm and huddled close to him to stay dry.

Inside, the police station was freezing. It didn't help that Jessica's thighs were wet. If she'd known she'd be visiting the station, she'd have worn her jeans instead of one of her grandma's vintage dresses. She liked to wear pants when confronting authority . . . or extreme air conditioning.

The waiting room was run-down and tired, with stained chairs, cracked floor tiles, and a chipped counter. The folks in the waiting room had also seen better days. A skinny man wearing baggy, soiled clothes clutched a plastic bag while an old lady dozed, her double chin on her chest. Harsh fluorescent lights gave everything a sharp edge. And the smell of rotten fruit mixed with sour wash-water was aggressive. She crinkled her nose.

Nick told the receptionist he had an appointment with Detective Cormier. A few minutes later, the detective appeared, wearing a smart-looking suit as always. He ushered them back through a long corridor to an office tucked away in a quiet corner of the building. *Hey, the detective didn't make me wait in the lobby. What a surprise!*

Unlike the rest of the station, Detective Cormier's office had new furnishings and was lit with soft floor lamps. He gestured toward a seating area with a leather couch and two matching chairs. *So, this isn't a formal interrogation, but a friendly conversation*, Jessica thought as she took a seat in one of the chairs. The leather was cool against her damp thighs, and she pulled her dress down over her knees.

"We've got the coroner's report on your father," Detective Cormier said, glancing over at Nick as he sat across from him on the couch.

When Nick raked his hand through his hair, his hand was shaking. He seemed more nervous than an innocent man should be. He peered at the detective expectantly.

"Did you know your father was taking digoxin for atrial arrhythmias?" Cormier asked.

"I knew he was taking some kind of heart medicine. He has been for a couple of years." Nick twisted the ring around his little finger.

"His blood contained four times his normal dose, possibly enough to cause a fatal cardiac arrest."

The color drained from Nick's face. "Why would he have taken four times his normal dose?"

"Unless he was given an overdose by someone else," Jessica added. She still suspected foul play.

"It's looking less like a case of accidental death and more like a case of suicide or murder," said the detective. He picked up a file folder from the coffee table. "That's not all. One of the tea cups we tagged at the scene contained traces of digoxin."

She knew it! "So, someone poisoned him?"

"Either that or he administered it to himself."

"Suicide?" Nick asked. "As I told you before, I doubt my father would kill himself. It doesn't make sense."

"Do you know of anyone who would want him dead?" the detective asked.

"Probably half of Manhattan," Nick said. "Seriously, given the way he did business, he made a lot of enemies."

"And what was his business?"

"Real estate . . . and a couple of nightclubs." Nick shifted in his chair. "But let's just say he dealt with unsavory characters and engaged in some pretty shady deals. I guess you might as well know he was chums with Victor Marsiano, otherwise known as 'Teeth.'"

"Teeth?" Jessica asked. Sounded like Nick's dad hung out with some shady characters.

"Don't ask," Nick glanced over at her and grimaced.

"So, your father did business with New York mafia bosses?" Detective Cormier was making notes on a legal pad.

Nick nodded. "I'm afraid so."

"Had he crossed any of his business associates lately?" The detective glanced up from his notes, his tawny eyes intent on getting answers.

"I wouldn't know. As I told you, my father and I weren't exactly close." Nick shoved a lock of hair away from his face.

Jessica had never seen him so nervous. She was worried. Even though they weren't close, he must be taking his father's death pretty hard.

"And yet he made a sizable donation to your Center." Detective Cormier clicked the top of his pen.

"True."

"And much of it wasn't actualized until his death."

"Also true." Nick stared down at his hands.

"So, you stood to benefit from his death."

"So it seems." He glanced up at the detective. "But I didn't kill him."

"Nick is innocent," Jessica chimed in. At least, she hoped he was.

"If he isn't, I'll find out," the detective said, dropping the pen on the desk and standing to escort them out. He left them at the front door. "I may need to talk to you again."

Nick nodded.

The rain had stopped, but Nick pulled Jessica close as they strolled back to the car. She should pull away, but she was scared. Her graduate career was hanging by a thread. One of her best friends might be involved in a murder. And the man she loved was a nervous wreck. Anyway, in spite of everything, it felt good to have Nick's body next to hers. She felt bad that it felt so good.

"What do you say to a drink before dinner?" he asked.

"More like a drink for lunch." Somehow she was involved in another murder case. She could use a drink. Anyway, she'd never been one to turn down a cocktail. "Why not?" She put her arm around his waist, determined to forget about overdue dissertations and murdered billionaires.

Maybe I don't need a drink. She was already drunk from the warmth of Nick's body so close to hers. Even through his light wool jacket, she could feel the heat of his skin. She shouldn't have thought of his skin, so tanned and smooth. He held her so close she had to synchronize her steps to avoid tripping. She inhaled his spicy scent and felt a powerful craving no drink could satisfy.

There was something especially delicious about skipping out of adult responsibilities to have fancy cocktails in the middle of the afternoon. Soon, nibbling on smoked almonds, she took in the midafternoon scene at one of Chicago's hottest mixology clubs. Three well-dressed business women sat at a high table, chatting animatedly and drinking blue-green martinis while another couple cuddled in a dark corner booth, sipping from the same tall glass. The Japanese cocktail bar was known as the most romantic spot for drinks in Chicago. With its rice paper screens, soft sconce lighting, and baby orchid centerpieces, Jessica could see why.

Jessica ordered a Jasmine Martini Float and Nick ordered a Sea Flower Martini, which promised to be served on the rocks with a rim of "ocean dust." She could eat for a week on the cost of those two drinks.

When the drinks arrived, Nick proposed a toast. "To you."

"To us!" She carefully held up her glass and clinked it against his. *To us?* She couldn't believe she'd just said that. *Am I starting another relationship with him? Is that what I'm doing?* She wasn't going to overthink it. She was just going to do it—be happy, for once. She focused on her drink. The jasmine-coconut concoction was a gorgeous cream color with a dollop of green genmaicha ice cream and a tiny pink orchid floating on top. She took a sip and tangy sweetness exploded in her mouth —dry gin, coconut cream, and a hint of lemon, along with the sharp green tea and toasted rice flavors of genmaicha. She closed her eyes to savor it. When she opened them again, Nick was staring at her.

"You ruined my life," he said, his intense eyes boring a hole in her soul. "Before I fell in love with you, I never considered my future. Now, I'm miserable because I simply can't imagine it without you in it." He extended his hand across the table and hers met it halfway.

Her heart was galloping, and she felt like she might throw up. She smiled and blushed but couldn't speak.

"What if I quit my job at the university? Would that make any difference?" The earnest look in his eyes told her he wasn't joking.

She retracted her hand. *Quit his job! Is he serious? He'd do that for her?* "I wouldn't want you to quit your job. That's crazy!"

"The only thing crazy is how much I love you." A lock of wavy hair fell across his forehead.

Oh. My. God. Her anxiety level shot through the

roof. "That's crazy." She sounded like a broken record. She could barely sit still. *Where is this going?*

"Think about it." His caress on her fingers sent sparks up her arm.

"Think about what?" She gulped down the rest of her drink waiting for the answer.

He took her hand in both of his. The intensity of his gaze made her uneasy. *Is he proposing or something?* She was especially interested in the *or something*.

"Never mind. Everything should be perfect. I'm getting ahead of myself." He stuttered. "Sorry. I lost my head."

She'd never seen the eloquent art history professor at a loss for words. He withdrew his hands, and she was desperate to touch him again.

"Would you like another?" he asked.

"I'll try the Falling Blossom." The name was appropriate.

"I've missed you." His intense gaze made her blush. "I think about you every day . . . and night."

She scooted her chair around the table until it was next to his. "I've missed you, too. It's weird, but when I was with you, I knew what I wanted and where I was going. Since then, I've been unmoored."

"I know what you mean," he said. He sipped his martini and then smiled. "I have an idea!"

"What?"

"It's a surprise." He looked like he'd just solved the riddle of the sphinx. "One more round, and then I'm taking you to a late lunch. At the very least, I owe you some banana pancakes."

"At the very least," she laughed.

"With syrup." He winked.

"And whipped cream." She bit her lip.

After they finished their second round of martinis, Nick took her by the hand and led her back out to the car. As he opened the passenger door for her, she caught a familiar blonde bob and slim form across the street. "Isn't that your intern, Sally what's-her-name, over there?"

"What's she doing here?"

"Following us?" Jessica had been suspicious of the twenty-something intern from the first time she'd laid eyes on her, with her smug smirk and wiggly hips.

Nick narrowed his brows. "Why would she do that?"

"She's jealous." Jessica poked him in the arm. "She wants you to herself."

Nick laughed. "She wants your job, more like."

THIRTY MINUTES LATER, Jessica was floored when Nick parked in front of a chic new vegan restaurant that had just opened up in the Loop. He must really care for her, sacrificing his steak. How did he even know about this place?

With its marble bar, candlelit tables, and soft jazz, High Garden was more like a cigar bar than Jessica's usual crunchy granola joints. The menu was just as alien . . . beluga lentil caviar and celeriac-and-potato rösti replaced veggie burgers and tofu stir-fry.

Over late lunch—or was it early dinner?—they fell into a conversation about one of Jessica's favorite subjects, Russian art. It was uncanny, but talking to Nick about Nietzsche's influence on the Blue Rider group seemed as natural as diving into Whitefish Lake on an August afternoon.

"Kandinsky's idea that the artist is on a mission to touch the souls of his viewers seems a tad bit arrogant, don't you think?" Nick asked, poking around his plate with his fork.

"But great art does touch the soul and change the way you look at the world. That's its power." She was enjoying the debate as much as she was the lentils and celery sauce.

"Great art is like a good meal." He pointed to her plate with his fork. "It touches the senses, but why demand more of it than that? When you do, it starts to sound like religion."

"Maybe we'd be better off if art replaced religion. With art, there's no punishing god—only the sublime experience of losing yourself in a painting or a song." She finished off her mushroom risotto. For the first time in a while, Jessica felt a flush of purpose. She actually looked forward to getting back to her computer. "This meal is a work of art. Thank you for bringing me here. I know it's not your kind of place."

"Your pleasure gives me pleasure," he said, smiling.

The waitress delivered dessert—flourless chocolate cake with vegan coconut frosting—along with two forks. Jessica was full, but that didn't stop her from digging in. *Yummy!* The dense cake, rich dark chocolate, and light, creamy coconut, was the perfect marriage of flavors and textures.

Nick glanced at his oversized watch. "I'm not looking forward to this meeting with Chrissy." He sighed.

"Your stepmother?"

He laughed. "She's younger than I am."

"Oh. That must be awkward." Jessica took a break from the rich dessert. "And she's a supermodel?" Chrissy better not make a play for him. *Wow*. She was jealous. What a weird feeling.

"She's a model. It's a good thing she can fall back on her looks, because if she had to live by her wits, she'd be in sorry shape." He called the waitress over and ordered an espresso. "She's not the brightest bulb in the pack. Her schemes are so transparent she might as well be see-through."

"Why does she want to see you?" Jessica asked, trying to sound nonchalant.

"I'm assuming it has something to do with my father's will. She was asking about it earlier. I hope she doesn't expect me to play the comforting stepson." He shook his head. "I really can't stand to be around her for more than ten minutes." He drained his espresso. "It's been quite a day. I'm pretty sure my dad was using the Center to launder money. Then one of the trustees called me, demanding I hire his daughter. And now Chrissy. I need moral support. Will you come with me?"

"To talk to Chrissy?" She glanced at her phone. *Crapulence!* They'd been talking and drinking for hours. Where had the day gone?

"To the Parker Hotel. You could wait for me while I meet Chrissy." He signed the credit card receipt. "Then we could have a drink after."

"I don't know. . ." She wanted him. She wanted him more than ever. But she shouldn't. She was so close to getting her degree—why screw it up now? *Damn. Why is he so hot?*

"I won't be longer than a half hour. And I have a surprise for you."

"You're full of surprises today." She raised her eyebrows.

He stood up. When he smiled down at her, his polished canines sent shivers up her spine.

"What kind of surprise?" she asked.

"Come along, Dolce." He held out his hand. "You'll see."

10

Amber couldn't believe that the day after Mr. Schilling was found dead with her tea bags in his room, she had to go back to the Parker Hotel. Sweating, she fidgeted in the seat of her car. The traffic was terrible on Lake Shore Drive. She hated driving. And she dreaded going back into that fancy hotel. Why'd her boss have to have a baby?

She thought of Gary—how cute their baby would be, if they ever had one. Maybe someday. She hoped. They'd talked about marriage but decided to wait until they both finished school.

Even though the university would reimburse her, Amber felt bad for parking in the thirty-dollar-a-day garage at the Parker. Her beat-up Toyota Corolla was out of place amongst the BMWs and Porsches. She drove to the last floor of the garage and parked in a dark corner. She checked her phone to see where she was supposed to meet the potential donor. Mrs. Vandermeer's late husband was an alum who had made it big in Silicon Valley after graduating with a major in Russian history, of all things.

Amber was better at dealing with computers than people, especially rich people. She'd been working for the development office for over a month and still wasn't used to the dollar amounts—and designer perfumes—floating through the department. She preferred healing essential oils to the ingredients used in rich ladies' perfumes. Some luxury brands contained castoreum and hyraceum—fancy names for beaver anal secretions and fossilized badger urine. Honestly, badger urine! I shouldn't even be here. Amber's boss was on maternity leave, and her boss's boss had just been headhunted by Harvard . . . leaving Amber in this awkward position. I'm a math whiz, not an estate planner.

Everyone said she'd been lucky to get this internship in the development office, especially since she was older than your typical college senior. She still cut hair on the side to make extra money . . . and because she loved it. She could tell a lot about a person by their hair. The way they cared for it, the way they styled it, even its texture told her something. Folks who wanted perfect hair were usually trying to make up for some insecurity in another area of their life. She had a theory: thick hair was for extroverts—like her—and thin hair was for introverts. And people who didn't care about their hair were deceiving themselves about something else.

She would probably still be doing hair full-time if it weren't for Gary convincing her she was a computer wizard—and, of course, her biological father leaving her that money in his will. He must have felt guilty about getting her mom pregnant all those years ago. She was glad she could go back to cutting hair if the computer science thing didn't work out. Hacking was fun, but programming was boring. She'd helped Jessica hack that Pope mafia guy a couple years ago. And she'd made the fake thumbprint Jack had used to break into the animal lab. Considering Jack was in prison, maybe that had been a mistake. But she'd rather help Jack liberate lab rats than meet rich donors. She needed the job to afford her tuition, so she really had no choice.

In the hotel elevator, Amber rifled through her purse until she found the reassuring blue vial. She dropped five drops of the pungent herbal tincture under her tongue. She tapped on the top of her head to rebalance her body's magnetic energy. Computer science might pay the bills, but natural healing was her true calling. She could spot a misaligned aura from ten feet away.

As she knocked on the hotel room door, she sensed a strong negative energy swirling like a vortex on the other side of the door. When the door opened, that toxic vortex materialized in the person of Mrs. Vandermeer, a tall reed of a woman with a perfectly painted face. With her Botox and lip fillers, Mrs. Vandermeer looked like all the other rich women donors Amber had met, except less stretched and puffy. She looked like a very well-preserved fifty-year-old but held her heart-shaped lips in the perpetual pout of a teenage girl.

Amber extended her hand. "I'm Amber Bush from the development office. I have the paperwork you already discussed with my colleague."

"Wonderful," Vandermeer gushed. "I'm looking forward to discussing my estate planning."

"I understand you're particularly interested in donating to the Center for Russian Art and Culture," Amber said, wondering why such a young-looking woman would be thinking about estate planning. Her hair was ash silver—*obviously a balayage, a very expensive one*—but everything else about her was vibrant and young.

"Yes, I just adore everything Russian." She gestured toward a small table. "I've ordered us tea."

"Thanks." Amber sat down and pulled a slightly bent folder out of her mammoth purse. "Here are the documents. Once you cut through the legalese, it's really very simple. If you'd like to will your estate to the Center, we can make sure it happens. Upon your death, the Center would receive the funds. We all appreciate your support." She'd had to practice her lines on how grateful the university was for financial support, how important their mission was, how the development office would make sure the funds were used appropriately. She felt like a robot on autopilot. She sat on her hands to keep from playing with her hair.

"I just sign these documents and that's it? And then it's all legal and binding?"

"Yes, sign them and return them in the white envelope." She fidgeted in the chair, hoping the meeting would be over soon. She needed more Rescue Remedy.

"What if I change my mind later?"

"You mean if you no longer want to leave your estate to the Center? You can always specify another recipient at the university." Amber spewed the spiel. "You could endow a chair in a specific department, or you could make a general donation and leave it up to the discretion of the administration—"

"What if I no longer want to donate?" Mrs. Vandermeer folded her hands in her lap. "How do I cancel this agreement?"

"You can cancel at any time. Just send a letter indicating you want to cancel—"

"What if I die and my heirs want to cancel the donation?"

Amber shifted in her chair. "I'm not sure. I think it depends on whether you put it in your will or just make the pledge." She wished her boss was here.

"So, if it is only a pledge, then it isn't binding and the wife—er, husband, wouldn't have to honor it?" She smiled.

"That's right. Only if it's in his will would it be binding. I guess you should check with your lawyer."

"Of course, I will." She smoothed her skirt. "Do most people do a pledge or also put it in their will?"

"I'm not sure. Depends on whether they want their heirs to be able to change the bequest, I guess." *Why is this rich lady asking so many questions? Does she want to donate or not?* Amber had a calculus test to study for.

Mrs. Vandermeer passed her a box containing an assortment of teas. "Would you care for tea?"

Just to be polite Amber took it. When their hands touched, she sensed that vortex of toxicity again. She shifted in her chair, itching to do her energy-balancing protocol. "You know what? I have my own tea." Amber reached in her pursed and pulled out a baggie full of homemade tea bags. "This is my special detox blend. It has peppermint, milk thistle, and chamomile . Very nourishing for the liver."

Mrs. Vandermeer tried to raise her botoxed eyebrows. "Mind if I try it?"

"You're welcome to keep all of it." Amber passed her the baggie. "Drink it a couple times daily. If the detox effect is too intense, back it down to once a day." She hoped these tea bags wouldn't meet the same fate as the last ones she'd shared with a VIPER donor.

Mrs. Vandermeer was very much alive when Amber left her, tea bags and all. On the way back to her car, she glanced at her phone. She had just enough time to stop by the Girls First Refugee Center and deliver school supplies for Amira, Lila, and the rest of the younger girls. She'd bought paints and a sketch pad for Amira. For the younger girls, she had colored pencils, Hello Kitty notebooks, and backpacks adorned with the princess sisters from *Frozen*. She hoped the girls would like them. After dropping off the supplies, she had to get back to campus for Gary's stupid Young Socialists meeting. Then she had to study for her calculus test, before going back to Girls First to teach her English night class for adult refugees. *What a day!* She fumbled in her purse for her Perk Up energy drops.

The Girls First headquarters was a red brick building in the heart of Rogers Park, not too far from her apartment. Amber had been working with the organization for two years now. She loved tutoring the younger girls, but their stories broke her heart. She had a soft spot for Amira, whose family had fled Syria when she was only four. After three years in a Turkish refugee camp, they'd made it to Chicago. Seventeen-year-old Amira refused to speak. Instead, she drew and painted pictures.

Amber parked her car, grabbed the shopping bag from the backseat, and hurried into the building. The sound of a commotion came from one of the classrooms. When she opened the door, she saw Amira crying in a corner.

"What's going on?" Amber asked the volunteer teacher.

"I told her to put her drawings away and pay attention to the lessons." The teacher huffed. "So, I took her pencils and paper away and she became hysterical."

Amber rushed to Amira and hugged her. "There, there, sweetie. You'll get them back." She wiped tears from the teenage girl's round face, then pulled a chocolate bar from her purse and held it out. "This will make you feel better." *This volunteer is bad news.* Amber would have to report her to the director.

Amira sniffed and sat up on her knees, her long dark braids falling over her shoulders. She tentatively reached for the candy. Amber nodded, and the girl grabbed the chocolate with a weak smile. Amber stroked her hair. Poor thing had seen so much violence. She'd had to watch her father murdered and her mother assaulted. No wonder she wouldn't talk.

If only there was something more Amber could do for these sweet girls . . .

11

It was surprisingly easy to persuade Jessica to wait for him in the hotel suite—as far away from the penthouse as he could get—while he went to meet Chrissy. Nick hoped that was a good sign. Maybe she felt the same way he did. His pulse quickened. He loved her with an overpowering urgency and it scared him. He'd given himself over to a lot of women, but he'd always been guarded with his heart—until Jessica. Something about her honesty, bordering on brutality, was irresistible. They'd only been together a month, and that was two years ago, but his feelings for her hadn't waivered. He'd known then that he loved her. He was even more certain of it now.

His plan to propose to her tonight was insane, but now he was obsessed. It just felt right. Since he'd hatched the plan a few hours ago, he'd felt happier than he had in a long, long time. She'd probably say no. But that was a chance he'd have to take. He knew he would never meet anyone else like her. She was so smart, and pretty, and real. He wanted her, yes. But he also wanted to share his life with her. Spending time with her again after two years apart had convinced him his life was meaningless without her. He was serious about quitting the university. He could devote himself to the Center. To making Jessica happy.

He glanced at his watch. He'd have to hustle to prepare for the dreaded meeting with Chrissy. First stop, the Cartier store in the hotel's mezzanine. He was rushing it, but his father's death made him realize you had to seize life while you could.

I'm thirty years old, he thought. *It's time*. He'd never wanted to get married. In fact, he'd sworn off the institution. So why did he want it so much now with Jessica? Something about her had changed him. He quickened his pace. He had to get to the store before it closed.

The jewelry store had low lights, just enough to show off the sparkling gems in its sparsely populated cases. Like predatory animals, each precious piece seemed to require its own territory.

"I'm looking for an engagement ring," he told the clerk. "Something unique."

He figured Jessica wouldn't like your usual giant diamonds in gaudy gold settings. Come to think of it, he'd never seen her wear a ring . . . or any jewelry, for that matter. Maybe she wouldn't like a ring. He considered getting her something else, but what? A necklace, a bracelet? A pin? He paced around the store, bending over case after case. Whatever he got, it had to be perfect.

The clerk brought out three rings to choose from. One was a large diamond in a simple setting, elegant but bold. The second had a diamond surrounded by rubies in a silver setting, pretty and different. The third was a jade ring with tiny diamonds all around the band. None of them looked like Jessica. He threaded his hand through his hair. He was running out of time. He had to find something and fast.

Still fingering the jade ring, he glanced around until a case of pocket watches caught his eye. He handed the ring back to the clerk and headed to the case. There—a gold watch with an onyx stem and diamond-studded hands. It wasn't a traditional engagement ring, but Jessica wasn't a traditional girl. "I'll take that," he said, greatly relieved. "And the ring."

The clerk stepped away, then returned with two small red velvet boxes, one smaller than the other.

Nick slipped them into his jacket pocket. On the way out the door, he spotted Sally Marshall peeking around the corner of the hallway. *What in the hell is she doing here?* If she weren't the daughter of the most important trustee, he just might fire her. But then, maybe Sally had her own assignation at the Parker. *Maybe it's just a coincidence she's here.* He'd worry about her later.

Nick set out for the registration desk, where he

ordered champagne and roses to be delivered to his suite at eight. He'd give Chrissy exactly thirty minutes, then rejoin Jessica. His heart skipped. He couldn't wait to see the look on her face. Even if she said no, it would be worth it. His plan was coming together. He'd managed to get a nice suite at the last minute, then a ring, and now roses. Everything had to be perfect.

He was tempted to blow off Chrissy and go straight back to Jessica. But he was a man of his word, and he'd promised to meet her. Just one drink. Then he'd be free. On the way to her room, he rehearsed his proposal.

Room 817. He knocked on the door. Chrissy answered, wearing a slinky red satin dress . . . or was it a slip? Whatever it was barely covered her Victoria's Secret assets. *Is my father's newly widowed wife coming on to me?* He had to get this over with and get back to Jessica before things got more awkward.

"Thanks for coming." She batted her eyelashes as she led him to a small sitting area. "I hope you don't mind—I ordered us some martinis. *Dirty*, just the way you like them." The way she said "dirty" turned his stomach. He knew it. She'd never loved his father. It had always been the money.

"Kind of you to remember," he said, doing his best to be polite. He took a seat across from her. "I can't stay long. Why did you want to see me?" Maybe if he was nice, he could get out sooner.

Chrissy dropped a toothpick loaded with olives into

a martini glass and handed it to him. "How did you do it?"

"Do what?"

"Get your father to change his will." She smoothed her dress.

"What do you mean?" Nick grimaced at the taste of his martini. He wasn't a fan of gin. She'd gotten the dirty part right, but not the alcohol. He always drank vodka martinis.

"You manipulated him into donating to your precious Center." She took a sip of her drink. "And leaving the rest to you."

He narrowed his eyes. "You're mistaken. I'd barely spoken to my father in years." He was confused. Was Chrissy playing some game with him? If she was telling the truth, his father must have had a huge con planned . . . but for after his death? It didn't make sense.

"Thanks to your conniving, I'm left out in the cold." She glared at him.

"*Excuse me?* I'm sure that's not true." She had some nerve accusing him of scheming. "Anyway, you have your modeling career."

"Victoria's Secret dropped me," she scoffed, waving a manicured hand. "Apparently, I'm too fat and too old."

Now he scoffed. "That's absurd. You're twenty-eight and gorgeous and you know it." *What is she up to?* He eyed her suspiciously.

"It's a cutthroat world." She wiped her eyes on the back of her hands, careful not to smear her makeup.

"I've lost my husband. I've lost my job. I've lost everything," she moaned.

Nick almost felt sorry for her. He took another sip, wondering what to do. Was this a trick, or had she really lost her job? He sat his drink on the coffee table and moved to sit beside her on the couch. "You'll be okay." He glanced at his watch. He had to calm her down and get back to Jessica.

When he patted Chrissy's hand, she leaned her head against his shoulder. Her proximity made him nauseous. He was sweating and dizzy. A searing pain shot through his chest.

"Not feeling well?" Chrissy asked, biting her lip.

He shook his head.

"Now, why don't you tell me what you did with the jewels?" She started unbuttoning his shirt, and he was helpless to stop her. He clutched his chest and whispered, "Dolce."

JESSICA'S COWBOY boots clicked on the marble floor as she paced back and forth in the suite. Nick had said he'd be back by seven thirty, and it was already nine. Obviously, he'd underestimated Chrissy's charms. She checked her phone. No messages. And it was only five minutes later than the last time she checked.

She flopped onto the couch and flipped on the television, forcefully ignoring her dissertation. After a couple of cocktails and an afternoon with Nick, she was hardly in the mood for dead philosophers. She studied the room service menu and considered ordering a cheese plate or some cookies. She wasn't really hungry, just impatient. Her appetite wasn't for food. She tapped her phone awake and texted Nick.

A knock at the door startled her. She jumped up and opened it, but her heart sank—no Nick, just room service. *But wait . . . I didn't order anything.*

"Roses and champagne," the porter said. "Should I put them on the table?"

She nodded. Nick must have ordered them when he realized he'd be late. *How sweet.* When the porter left, she texted Nick a thank-you. She inhaled the sweet smell of two dozen red roses and twirled the champagne bottle around in the bucket of ice.

There was another knock. *Room service again?* She opened the door. *What the . . .* Nick's intern, Sally what's-her-name, was standing in the doorway, arms akimbo. She looked like she'd stepped out of a Grace Kelly movie, wearing tight capri pants and a pressed linen blouse, dripping with diamonds.

"So, you and Nick are having a fling?" Sally pushed past her and marched into the room. "Not very professional, are you?"

"What are you doing here?" Jessica followed her into the suite. "What do you want?"

"I want you to stay away from Nick." Sally's glare

seethed with privilege. "He's mine and so is the job as assistant director."

"What are you talking about?"

"I've worked my ass off for that position."

"I bet you have." *Is there something between Nick and this spoiled brat?* Jessica swallowed hard. She felt like kicking the nasty little weasel in the shin.

"Daddy promised—" Sally yanked a rose out of the vase. "Never mind." And with that, she stormed out of the room.

Jessica's chest was buzzing as she sat on the couch, staring at the flowers. Waiting. The intern's visit had set her on edge. None of this seemed right. Why was she waiting in this hotel room for a man she could never have?

She texted Nick again and kept her phone in hand, waiting for his reply. Fifteen minutes and still nothing. She texted him again. Another fifteen minutes went by. She grabbed the remote and switched the channel on the TV. After channel surfing for another half hour, she picked up the hotel telephone, her finger hovering over the button for reception. She chickened out and dropped the receiver back in its cradle. Then she hopped off the couch and went to the minibar.

The little bottles reminded her of her first time on an airplane, back when she left Montana for grad school. So much had changed since then.

When she first got to Chicago, she'd never been in a big city, never seen a foreign film, never eaten Thai food, and never been in love. Over the last four years, she'd learned a lot, most of it outside of the classroom. As one of only two girls studying philosophy in the entire PhD program, and probably the only student from a Montana trailer park, Jessica felt out of place. Her fellow grad students came from Ivy League schools and grew up eating Brie and water crackers. They thought SPAM was what you found in your junk mail folder, not breakfast. Given her background, Jessica felt lucky just to speak proper English, let alone French or German.

Her phone buzzed and she leapt for it. *Finally!*

"Cowgirl! I'm glad you answered." The familiar smoky voice surprised her.

"Jack." She tried not to sound disappointed.

"Why didn't you visit last weekend? I miss you."

"Things have been crazy. The department has given me until the end of the semester to finish my dissertation or I'll get kicked out."

"Harsh."

"Yeah." She should be working on it now instead of waiting for Nick to come back from the supermodel's room. Why couldn't she focus? *Duh.* Because the hottest man on the planet wanted to spend the night with her . . . if Chrissy didn't seduce him first.

"Good news!" Jack chuckled. "Looks like I'm getting out for good behavior. Could be as early as next week. I just found out, and I'm friendly with the warden—that's how I got to make this call."

"That's wonderful." What a relief. She'd felt so guilty about his prison sentence. "Let me know when and I'll be there." A tingling sensation in her stomach confused her.

"You'll be the first person I call. Gotta go. My time's up." Jack sighed. "I love you."

She blew at her bangs. "I know. Me too." She did love him as a friend, and she'd missed him terribly. Anyway, what was she going to say to the guy stuck in a prison cell?

She needed a drink. She grabbed a couple tiny bottles of Jack Daniels and a Coke from the minibar. She popped the soda tab, pouring the whiskey straight into the can.

The carbonation hit her tongue first, followed by the sweet caramel combo of whiskey and coke. She dropped back onto the couch, threw her legs over its arm, and checked her phone. Still no word from Nick. After another few gulps, she unscrewed the second little bottle and added it to the can. *Just to calm my nerves.* It was absurd, but the thought of Nick with supermodel Chrissy made it hard to breathe.

She glanced at the time. It was almost eleven. *Damn it to hell! Where is he?* She went back to the desk and picked up the telephone receiver again. Before she had time to think about it, she punched the button for reception.

"Can I help you, Mrs. Schilling?" asked the woman on the other end.

Being called "Mrs. Schilling" gave Jessica a start. She almost hung up. She took a deep breath and asked, "Can you connect me to Chrissy Schilling's room, please?"

She heard typing on the other end. "What was the name? Can you spell it?"

"Schilling," she repeated. "S-C-H-I-L-L-I-N-G."

"I'm sorry, Mrs. Schilling, but we don't have another room under that name."

WTF? What was going on? "Check again."

"I'm sorry. There's no guest by that name."

So, the flowers were just a consolation prize?

Jessica hung up. With tears in her eyes, she downed the rest of the Coke, grabbed her jacket and book bag, and took off for home. As her mother would say, "Best to cut your losses while you still can." She knew Nick was a player, but she'd never figured him for a liar. Then again, it wasn't like they were really together.

Outside, the air was heavy with humidity. Even in the middle of the night, it was hot and sticky. Something about the darkness made it even worse. By the time she reached the train stop, she was sweating.

Friday night on the "L" was raucous with businessmen coming home late from extended happy hours and teens heading out to start their weekend parties. The crowded train made her feel lonelier. She texted Lolita: *meet at Pavlov's?* A few seconds later her phone pinged.

@ poker game. Join us.

Usually, Lolita had to drag Jessica to those high-stakes games. Even though she was pretty darned good at poker, playing made her nervous—especially when the ante was as much as her yearly stipend. But tonight, she needed the distraction.

Where?

Parker Hotel. Presidential Suite.

Crapulence. She should have texted Lolita from the hotel. She'd have to get off at the next stop and turn back around. *See u in 15.*

Jessica retraced her steps to the Parker. Lolita sent a busty cocktail waitress down to the lobby to escort her up to the Presidential Suite . . . nothing but the best at the Poker Tsarina's games. She cringed to think of Lolita's usual spot, the Penthouse. It was probably still surrounded by yellow police tape.

The Parker Hotel was like a magnet, always drawing Jessica back. She hoped she wouldn't run into Nick. She also knew that wasn't true. She'd give anything to run into Nick, even if he *had* decided to spend the night with Chrissy.

As usual, Lolita had the suite set up with two poker tables, a full-top shelf bar, a side table laid out with fancy finger foods, and two gorgeous girls seeing to the needs of every high roller. The room stank of cigar smoke, expensive cologne, and money. Lots of money.

Jessica scanned the buffet for veggie options and loaded a plate with what she hoped were mushrooms in fancy puff pastry. In an attempt to look sophisticated, she sacrificed her usual Coke and poured herself a Gentleman Jack on the rocks. She sat on a couch, watching the games from afar, drowning her sorrow in the crunch of flaky pastry and the slow burn of whiskey.

She recognized some of the usual players: Vance Hamm, the skinny little actor who drank carrot juice and whined when he didn't win; the Chicago Bulls player who was better on the court than at the table; and a businessman she thought she'd seen somewhere before . . . She couldn't be sure, though. *They all look alike.*

There was one new guy, a bearded, craggy-faced chain-smoker. He seemed vaguely familiar—something about the slant of his sage-green eyes. If Jessica didn't know better, she would have suspected he was mafia. But given Lolita's history, the Poker Tsarina didn't allow mobsters at her games, no matter how much money they dropped.

Jessica studied the new guy from afar. She just couldn't shake the uncanny feeling she'd met him before. She'd seen those eyes. She watched as Lolita jumped every time the newcomer asked for something. He must be her latest high-rolling, high-tipping mark. But something about him gave Jessica chills. Who was he? And why's he so important to Lolita?

When the players broke for a midnight snack, Lolita introduced Jessica to the gang.

"I don't think we've met," Jessica said to the craggy-faced man.

"No. I've just arrived in Chicago," he replied in a thick Russian accent.

"Are you one of Lolita's second cousins?" She thought of Vanya, with his Italian lace-ups and designer lighter. "Or the mysterious uncle, returned from the dead?" She laughed at her own joke.

"That's our little secret." He gave her a wicked grin. "Sergei, Sergei Yudkovich." He extended his hand. "But you can call me Sly."

His grip was crushing, and she bit her lip to keep from yelping. "Jessica, Jessica James." She glanced over at Lolita, who was pouring drinks and purring endearments to the other players. Her friend returned her gaze and gave a furtive nod. What was the Poker Tsarina up to? She was definitely working some angle.

"You're Lolita's uncle?" She narrowed her eyes and stared into his face, looking for a resemblance. Then it struck her. Those sage-green eyes staring back at her were the very same uncanny cat eyes as Lolita's.

12

It was Sunday, just after midnight. Dmitry sat in the dark, waiting until the security guard finished his rounds. The glow of Vanya's cigarette throbbed from across the room. Couldn't his cousin go one hour without smoking? There would be a pile of spent cigarette butts waiting for him on the office floor in the morning.

"When do we snag them pictures?" Vanya tapped a cigarette out of his pack and flipped it into his mouth.

"Not until we're sure of the guard's routine." Dmitry took a small notebook and pen from his jacket pocket.

"What about them cameras?" The unlit cigarette bobbed up and down.

"That's where you come in. When the guard is out on his next rounds, you'll hack the surveillance system to play a loop of the empty galleries."

"Nice. What about alarms?" He played with his lighter.

"They're installing them on Tuesday." Dmitry headed for the office door. "The heist is Monday night."

"Tomorrow?" Vanya stopped clicking his lighter and stared.

"That's what Sergei says." Dmitry sighed. "He's joining us."

Vanya smirked. "I still can't believe he's alive after all these years." He chuckled. "He always did have a way of turning up like a bad benny."

"Bad *penny*," Dmitry said, absentmindedly. He remembered the time Sergei had tied him to a tree on top of an ant nest. Just thinking about it made his skin crawl. Sergei thrived on violence and devoured other people's fear. He'd always been a sadist.

"Sly always did like to get his hands dirty." Vanya fiddled with his lighter.

"Filthy, more like," Dmitry said under his breath. He couldn't believe that dirty *blyad* had the nerve to come to his house, sit at his kitchen table, and threaten his wife and daughter. He balled his fingers into fists and swore to protect his family, with his life if necessary. He only hoped his plan worked. If it didn't, he wouldn't live to get a second chance.

The seconds stretched into minutes. Dmitry checked his watch. Another ten minutes and the guard should be back at his desk. It seemed like hours.

Vanya dropped a cigarette butt on the floor and

ground it out under his Italian lace-up. He tapped another out of the pack and flipped it into his mouth. The click of his titanium lighter broke the silence.

Dmitry closed his eyes, waiting. *How did I get myself into this situation?* The smell of Vanya's smoke was getting under his skin.

"Put that out," he whispered.

"Sure thing, boss." Vanya crushed the cig with his heel. "Still I can't believe. Sly shows up here and takes over Bratva without even me knowing it. Guess I've been slacking off."

"Shhh!" Dmitry held his finger to his lips.

"I heard someone new come in a couple weeks ago and busted up some of the *vory*." Vanya chuckled. "But I'd never guessed in a million years it was old Sly."

"Be quiet!" Dmitry stage-whispered. Two more minutes until the guard finished his rounds. "Let's go." Dmitry came around his desk and walked on the balls of his feet to his office door. He slowly opened it, peeked out, and gestured to Vanya.

Vanya was right behind him as he crept down the hallway. Dmitry stopped behind a pillar, poked his head around it, and peered down into the gallery. From his vantage on the second-floor balcony, he could see down into the first-floor galleries. The one security guard on duty would be back at his desk, keeping an eye on the security camera footage.

"You take the hallway on that side of the pillar." Dmitry pointed. "And I'll take this side."

"Right, boss." When Vanya flashed him a smile, his gold grill reflected the dim lights of the Center.

"Watch out for the security guard. If you see him, duck back behind the pillar." Dmitry couldn't believe he was casing the place. If he got caught, he'd lose more than his job.

"You got it." Vanya was clearly enjoying this. Even as a kid, he couldn't stay out of trouble. Dmitry thought of the time when seven-year-old Vanya snuck into the pantry and ate all of the jam tarts. Cook had made them for a large dinner party Dmitry's mother was having for the city fathers. Vanya was sick all night, and Dmitry's mother had to serve Guriev porridge to the politicians in his father's pocket.

The sound of footfalls from the gallery below put Dmitry on high alert. He pressed himself up against the pillar. The guard had already made his rounds. Why was he in the galleries again now? He glanced at his watch and made a mental note of the time: twelve thirty. *Blyad!* He must have miscalculated the guard's schedule. He gritted his teeth.

The guard was whistling as he strolled through the galleries. Dmitry shut his eyes and trained his ears on the shrill melody. He knew the museum's layout so well that he could see a mental blueprint of its galleries. He traced the guard's path through the museum in his mind.

Dmitry heard the footfalls on the stairs. He moved around the pillar and crawled down the hallway to where his cousin was stationed. He tapped Vanya on the shoulder.

Vanya jumped and pulled a gun out from under his linen jacket. "Don't sneak up, boss. You scared me out of my tits!"

"*Wits.*" Dmitry should have known better than to ask his trigger-happy cousin for help. He hoped Vanya didn't accidently shoot someone. "We'd better get back to my office. Come on."

With Vanya hot on his heels, Dmitry slid down the hallway and ducked back into his office, locking the door. He pressed himself up against the wall on one side of the door and motioned for Vanya to do the same on the other side. Breathless, they listened to the footfalls approaching from the hall. Dmitry had messed up before the heist even started. Now, he was about to get caught casing his own place of employment.

His heart was racing. Hiding in the shadows with a pistol-wielding thug brought it all back—the trauma of Moscow. He thought he'd escaped the family business when he'd boarded that train to Riga, twenty-three years ago. But he was wrong. Deep down, he knew he'd never escape. His bloodstained past would haunt him for the rest of his life. Even if he did this "one thing," Sergei wouldn't disappear forever . . . not unless Dmitry killed him. Stealing the paintings was just a bid for time.

Vanya clicked his lighter.

"Put that away," Dmitry hissed. He strained to hear

any sounds coming from the hallway. All he heard was the hum of the air conditioner. The guard must have gone back downstairs.

"Dude's gone," Vanya said, an unlit cigarette dangling from his lip. He flipped the lid on his lighter and lit his cigarette.

"Really, do you need to smoke?"

A hurt look crossed Vanya's face. He took a drag, then pinched the end of the cigarette between his thumb and forefinger and slid it back into the pack. "What's Sly want with them pictures?" he asked.

"Those paintings are worth millions. The Kandinsky alone is valued at over thirty million." He tugged at his shirt collar.

Vanya whistled through his teeth. "Who'd pay millions for blobs of paint?"

Dmitry shook his head and shrugged. His cousin didn't appreciate art. Neither had Dmitry's father. For Anton, art was merely an investment in prestige, a way to impress Moscow's high society.

"Why don't you sell your paintings for millions, boss?"

"Because I'm not Kandinsky." He scowled at his cousin.

"But your pictures look just like his." Vanya was hopping from foot to foot. The wiry thug never could hold still.

"That's because they're copies, like the rest of my life."

"Lolita's an original and prettier than any picture." His cousin grinned.

Lolita. A clamp tightened around Dmitry's heart. He was doing his brother's bidding to protect Lolita. But with Sergei in town—with Sergei *anywhere*—his daughter would never be safe.

13

Jessica's hangover must have made her a better teaching assistant, or maybe it slowed down her brain to their speed, because after class, three students came up to say they finally understood modal logic. *Maybe I should teach with a hangover every day.* She'd been drinking all weekend, ever since Nick stood her up Friday night. Her head hurt so bad she wore her sunglasses in class.

Monday mornings were always tough. And this morning, Jessica needed something stronger than Witch's Brew. She stopped at Starbucks for a double-caramel iced macchiato and then headed for Blind Faith to get back to work on her dissertation. Her head was pounding, and her stomach hurt. But her heart hurt worst of all. How could Nick have ghosted her like that? She'd thought he was "the one." *What a jerk!*

The brutal sun was poaching her brain. It was way

too hot for September, but there were only so many clothes she could take off. Give me the coldest Montana winter to this Midwestern humidity any day. She sipped her cool, sweet coffee and trudged up the sidewalk toward the café. It was only a fifteen-minute walk from campus, but today it seemed to take forever. She felt like she might pass out.

She stopped under the shade of an awning and leaned against the cool brick building. Slurping the last of her macchiato, she thought of Nick's smooth forearms and soft lips. How could she have been such an idiot? She felt like barfing. Fighting tears, she forced herself to keep walking. She had to forget about Nick and get back to her dissertation.

The door to the café seemed heavier than usual. She strained to pull it open. Today, the smell of tamari and seaweed turned her stomach. To top it off, someone was sitting at her usual corner booth. She went to the counter and swiveled on a barstool. *Pancakes.* She needed pancakes. She ordered her usual short stack and bottomless cup of coffee. Maybe the sugar and extra caffeine would jump-start her brain.

She was just digging in to her pancakes when her phone buzzed. She savored the sweet cake and crunchy pecans for another second before picking up.

"Detective Cormier. What a surprise." *Of course.* She'd never get to eat her damned pancakes in peace.

"Can you meet me at the Parker Hotel?" the detective asked. "It's a matter of some urgency."

"I guess so. Why? What's happened?" Her heart leapt into her throat. She'd had enough of the snooty Parker Hotel and two-timing Nick Schilling.

"How soon can you get here?"

"It will take me at least forty-five minutes." *If I don't eat my pancakes.*

"Come to Room 817. I'll be waiting." He hung up.

Jessica scraped her pancakes into a to-go box and poured the coffee into a large paper cup, topping it with a good two inches of cream and a couple packets of sugar. She'd need all the help she could get to make it downtown. On her way out, she grabbed some plasticware and napkins. She'd have to eat her breakfast on the train.

THE TRAIN'S crush of bodies and lack of air conditioning made Jessica woozy. She sat crammed between a muscular dude with dreadlocks and headphones who took up more than his share of the seats and an overweight woman wearing a headscarf. Jessica held the cardboard to-go box with both hands but couldn't face the contents.

Crapulence! What could Detective Cormier want with her? Had he discovered she'd taken a picture at the crime scene? Or that she was carrying on her own investigation, as inconclusive as it was? She gulped her coffee, trying to jolt her brain awake. She didn't want to face the detective in this hungover fog.

The pitching and lurching of the train increased her nausea. She had to get off. Even though she was only halfway to the Parker, she jumped off at the next stop. On the platform, she sucked in air and hunted for a trash can. She'd lost her appetite. She dropped her empty coffee cup and pancakes into the trash, then hurried down the stairs to the street. A few blocks of walking helped clear her head, but the heat and humidity were oppressive. She gave up and called a Lyft. She'd already maxed out her credit card, but Lyft didn't know that yet. Her phone said her ride was two minutes away.

By the time she reached the Parker, she was exhausted. Between Nick ghosting her, the late-night poker game, her hangover, and her early morning class, she was completely undone. She longed to crawl back into bed and pull the covers over her head. She should have known better than to get involved with Nick again. A fist squeezed her heart and she nearly doubled over from the pain. She caught her breath, stumbled into the elevator, and pushed the button for the eighth floor. Panting, she leaned against the wall. *Why does loving him hurt so much?*

As she exited the elevator, she wondered if Nick was still here with Chrissy. She hoped she didn't run into him. *Why?* Why had he done it? She never had understood men, and she probably never would. *I should stick to horses.* Maybe they were wild animals, but they were easier to tame. For a sugar cube or a piece of black licorice, Mayhem would do anything she asked. She smiled. She missed her black beauty. If she did have to go back to Montana with her tail between her legs, at least she'd have her horses . . . and the mountains . . . and a fifth of vodka in the freezer and a bottle of Xanax on the nightstand.

She blew at her bangs and knocked on the door of Room 817.

"Miss James." Detective Cormier stepped out into the hallway. "Before you enter the room, I'm afraid I have some bad news."

Jessica felt the blood drain from her face and her stomach lurched. "Nick," she said under her breath. I should have known . . . when he didn't show up—"

"Yes. I'm afraid Professor Schilling is dead."

The words gutted her. "No, no, no." Jessica fell back against the wall and slid to the floor. "It can't be. I just . . ." She couldn't believe it. She'd just gotten him back, only to lose him forever. She wanted to scream.

"I'm sorry." Cormier reached down and pulled her to her feet.

Tears burst from her eyes. It felt like a team of Clydesdales had stomped on her chest. She leaned her head against the detective's shoulder. He smelled of shaving cream and peppermint, so different from Nick's citrus and juniper scent. *Nick.* How could he be dead?

He'd been so young and alive the last time she'd seen him.

After crying a puddle onto the detective's lapel, she wiped her nose on her shirtsleeve. He handed her a tissue from his pocket and she blew her nose.

"How did it happen?" she asked weakly, brushing tears from her cheeks with the back of her hands.

"Come sit down." The detective opened the door to the room and gestured her inside.

The room had the same sweet lavender and patchouli smell as Nick's father's suite. *Amber. WTF?* Jessica quickly scanned the room. A tea tray sat on an end table in the small sitting area. She hightailed it across the room and stood staring at the tea cups. At the bottom of each cup sat one of Amber's homemade linen tea bags, like desiccated flowers left too long without water. *What did Amber do? How could she?* Jessica shook her head. Her imagination was running away with her. No way Amber was capable of killing anyone. And even if she was, she had no reason to murder Nick or his dad.

"I suspect we will find digitalis in those cups," Cormier said. "This looks to be the same perpetrator as the one who killed Richard Schilling."

"Why?" Jessica asked. "Why would someone kill Nick or his dad?"

"If we knew the answer to that question, the case would be closed. He gestured toward the couch. "Please, have a seat. I'd like to ask you a few questions if you're up to it."

Jessica nodded.

"When was the last time you saw Nick Schilling?"

"Last night." She twisted the fringe on her jacket. "I was waiting for him in a suite while he went to meet his father's wife, Chrissy. But he never came back." She choked on the words.

"The wife was here?" Detective Cormier took out his notepad and started writing.

"She had stopped by earlier at the Center and asked Nick to meet at seven. Nick and I had dinner and drinks beforehand. He said he wouldn't be gone more than thirty minutes. I waited until almost midnight. I thought he'd stood me up . . ." Her voice trailed off.

"This room is registered to a 'Nicholas Charis.' It has been for the last week. That's Nick, right? Do you know why he had a room at the Parker?" He gave her an apologetic look.

"What?" Jessica shook her head. "Then why would he get another room last night?" None of this made sense. Her teeth were chattering. She buttoned her jacket up to the collar. "How did you find him?"

"A maid found him slumped over a chair at the table. I didn't want you to see that, so I waited to contact you until after we could move the body." Detective Cormier tightened his lips.

Jessica buried her head in her hands, weeping.

"The coroner puts the time of death sometime between seven and nine last night. Again, it looks like a heart attack. But I suspect the autopsy will turn up an overdose of digoxin. You can't think of anyone who might have wanted Professor Schilling dead?"

She shook her head. It sounded odd to hear Nick called "Professor Schilling." At the university, he was "Professor Charis." She remembered him in his office the first time she met him there . . . so animated and beautiful. She started crying again.

"I'm sorry to put you through this. But I need to know every detail of your movements yesterday."

As Jessica recounted the wonderful afternoon and evening, her heart contracted. She couldn't believe he was gone forever. *What if he was the love of my life?* She blew her nose.

"What did you do after he left to meet Mrs. Schilling?"

"I just waited in the suite. I watched a little television and had a whiskey from the minibar. When Nick wasn't back at ten, I started to worry. I called reception looking for Chrissy Schilling's room, but the operator told me she wasn't registered at the hotel." She dabbed at her eyes with the soggy tissue. "He sent flowers and champagne."

"No one has seen Mrs. Schilling for the last three days. We checked with her modeling agency. We'll find her." The detective closed his notebook and slid it inside his jacket.

"Do you think she killed Nick?" Jessica felt like she might barf.

"The only lead we have at this point are those teacups and the same odd-looking tea bags."

Jessica nodded. Amber's tea bags were now the primary lead in two murder cases. The love of her life was dead, and her friend was a suspect. *How did this happen?* The burning in the pit of her stomach spread to her chest.

"Wait. Nick's intern was here. She barged in and told me to stay away from Nick." Jessica sniffed. "Maybe she did it. She was jealous . . ." She broke down, crying.

"Tell me more about this intern." Detective Cormier held took his notebook back out of his pocket. "What's her name?"

"Sally something."

"We'll find her."

The detective removed two small red boxes from a sealed plastic bag. "Do you recognize these?"

Jessica shook her head.

He opened the boxes and sat them on the coffee table in front of her. "We found these in Nick's pocket. Apparently, he just bought them yesterday at the jewelry store downstairs. Do you know who he might have bought them for?"

Speechless, she stared at the perfect pocket watch and the beautiful jade ring. *Were those for me? Or for her?*

"There must be a link between the professor's death and his father's. Let me know if anything occurs to you." The detective stood up. "Maybe it's just a coincidence he was drinking tea before his death, but we don't have much else to go on at this point."

No way Amber's tea bags were a coincidence. *She has* something *to do with all of this. But what?*

"I was hoping you could give us more information," Cormier sighed. "You're free to go, but please let me know if you leave town."

"Am I a suspect?"

"As far as we know, you were one of the last to see him alive."

Her heart sank into her stomach. She wrapped her arms around herself and swayed back and forth. Forget about the dissertation. Forget about the degree. She had to find out who killed Nick and why.

14

The next morning, Jessica woke up hungover—this time not from whiskey, but from crying. She could barely open her puffy lids. She'd cried so much her pillow was still damp and her eyes were bone dry. She felt like she'd been run over by a logging truck.

She should have stopped Nick from going to meet Chrissy, *if* that's where he went. If she'd seduced him into spending the night with her, he'd still be alive. She turned over on her stomach and buried her head under her pillow. It hurt to breathe.

She couldn't face her logic class, so she called Donnette—department secretary and Amber's mother—and asked her to put a sign on the classroom door saying she was sick. Anyway, it was true. She *was* sick . . . heartsick. She could barely get out of bed, which was just a futon mattress on the floor in a corner.

The futon took up a good quarter of her tiny efficiency apartment. She didn't even have a proper kitchen, just a pint-sized fridge and hotplate in a closet, and she did her dishes in the bathtub. With clothes and papers strewn everywhere, her room was her messy, little nest. She was safe in the clutter, where she could burrow like a mouse to hide from the big, scary world.

"Brown bottle flu?" Donnette asked.

"Nick Charis died," Jessica whispered into the phone.

"Oh—I'm so sorry. Professor Charis was so young."

"Yeah. Looks like a heart attack." She didn't want to explain to Donnette that her daughter Amber's tea bags were found at the scene.

"Sure, honey, I'll leave a note on the door," Donnette drawled in her Texas accent. "Do you want me to stop by with some chicken soup? I can bring you some after work."

"No thanks." She didn't have the heart to remind Donnette that she was a vegetarian. Donnette was of a generation where chicken was considered a vegetable.

"What's new at the department?" Jessica asked to distract herself. A consummate gossip, Donnette was sure to have some story or other.

"Well, did you know that shifty Russian janitor left for some bigwig job downtown?"

Jessica closed her eyes and listened to the soothing sounds of Donnette's lilting voice jabbering on about Donnette's nemesis, Dmitry. She pictured Donnette in one of her matching sweater skirt sets, poking her big Texas hair with a long, spiky fingernail.

"You must be glad he's gone since you never liked him," she said in a daze.

"I liked him well enough. I just didn't trust him. Always skulking around the hallways . . . spending hours in the janitor's closet, painting. Who does that?"

"He's an artist at heart." Jessica kept her eyes closed, responding on autopilot just to keep Donnette talking. She didn't want to hang up.

"He's a communist from Russia."

"Not all Russians are communists." She inhaled a deep breath through her nose, held it, then blew it out her mouth.

"Maybe not, but that doesn't mean he isn't a shifty bastard." Donnette snorted.

Jessica thought of her logic class. *All Russians are communists. Dmitry is a Russian. Therefore, Dmitry is a communist.* "Maybe you can fill in for me today." She smiled, imagining the full-figured Texan in front of her class.

"Honey, you're a hoot. I'd rather eat a flying cockroach than stand up in front a room full of people."

"At this point in the semester, the room is hardly full." She rolled over on her side.

"You've scared them all away with your big brain."

"Bored them to death, more like." Jessica sat up in bed and leaned her head against the wall.

"I'd better go put up that sign before your students wonder where you are."

"Thanks, Donnette. You're the best." She meant it. Donnette may nag and pick, but she was loyal—the only person Jessica really trusted in Brentano Hall. "Hey, do you know what Amber's up to today?" She wasn't ready to get off the phone. Asking about Amber always got a rise out of her mother.

"That girl never tells me what she's doing. You'd think she'd have more concern for her poor old mom," Donnette huffed. "Since she started dating that good-for-nothing, she thinks she's hot stuff."

"You know that's not true. She's just busy." Phone in one hand, Jessica crawled out of bed and sat on the floor. "You should be proud of her. She's a computer whiz, and now she's working for the development office. She's got a promising career." *Unless she's lost her mind and started poisoning people with those disgusting herbal concoctions of hers.* "Why don't you like Gary?" she prodded.

"He's worse than the Russian, with his Young Communists." Donnette sighed heavily into the phone. "Why can't she find a nice Young *Republican*?" For Donnette, there was nothing in between: if you weren't a Young Republican, you were a communist.

"It's Young *Socialists*," Jessica corrected.

"Socialists, communists, what's the difference?" Donnette griped into the phone.

"I think Gary is a Democratic socialist. Like capitalism, socialism refers to the economy—whereas, like democracy, communism is a form of governance." Jessica couldn't help falling into teacher mode.

"Alright, smarty-pants. But I still don't trust him. He has shifty eyes and never smiles. Plus he's a socialist. And a communist."

Jessica wasn't in the mood to debate. She just wanted a distraction from her grief. "You're probably right—"

"I *know* I'm right. I hope you're not going to join those kooks too."

Jessica changed the subject. "The department gave me until the end of the semester to finish or I'm out."

"You'd better get to work, then, and so should I. No more goofing off, Little Miss. Sit your butt down and write your dissertation. Just do it."

Jessica knew this was Donnette's way of saying she had confidence in her. "Thanks, Donnette." At least someone in the department had her back, even if it was a bossy, big-haired Texan.

"Honey, make yourself a nice big cup of coffee and then get to work," Donnette said in a softer tone. "Work is the best medicine for grief. And if you see Amber, tell her to call me."

"I will."

After she hung up, Jessica threw on the same clothes she'd worn the day before and galloped down the stairs, out the front door, and down the street. With her long, quick strides, she cruised down the three blocks to Amber's apartment.

Amber's usual perky voice answered the buzzer. "Yes? Who is it?"

"It's me. Let me in." Jessica grasped the door handle, waited for the buzz, then dragged herself up the three flights of stairs, all the while wishing she had a strong cup of coffee.

She knocked on the door.

Amber answered holding a piece of toast, a dab of avocado on her upper lip. "I can't visit now," she said with her mouth full. "I've got to get back down to the Parker Hotel for work."

Jessica wiped the green blob off Amber's lip, then pushed the door open and headed for the kitchen.

Amber lived in a beautiful old apartment from the 1920s. It had glass doorknobs, hardwood floors, a fireplace in the living room *and* the bedroom—though neither worked—and cut-glass chandeliers. After her slimy bio-dad, Professor Wolfgang Schmutzig, died and left her some money, Amber had moved from her crummy studio on Howard to a nice apartment around the corner from The Heartland Café, one of Jessica's favorite vegetarian hangouts (after Blind Faith, of course). She wished she'd stopped there and gotten an organic soy latte.

Jessica turned on the tap and held her finger under the running water. "What are you doing at the Parker?"

"I'm meeting another donor. I still have to review

the files and get ready, so you can't stay long." Amber took a bite of her avocado toast. "Help yourself to some tea. The kettle is hot."

"Is it safe? I've heard your tea kills people." Jessica wiped her wet hand off on her jeans.

Amber gaped like a trout pulled out of Whitefish Lake.

"Did you have tea with Nick on Friday evening?" Jessica shot the question at her friend.

"Your Nick? No. Why would I—"

"Your tea bags were found in his hotel room."

Amber's brow crinkled. "I don't know what you're talking about."

"Parker Hotel. Two cups. Two of your chamomile tea bags."

Amber blinked.

"I recognized them. The same tea bags I took from Nick's father's suite the day he died."

"Those are my special blend, not just chamomile."

"So, you admit you were with Nick?"

"Why are you badgering me? I told you no." She plopped down on a barstool and dropped her toast onto a plate.

"Yesterday morning, a maid found Nick dead. Your teabags were there."

"*Your* Nick?"

"Yes," Jessica's voice broke. "My Nick." She fought back tears.

"He's dead?" Amber gasped and her hand flew to

her mouth. "Oh, poor dear. I'm so sorry." She disappeared into the other room and returned with her mammoth purse. "Open."

Jessica opened her mouth, and Amber dropped some sour liquid onto her tongue.

"Rescue Remedy. It will help calm you down."

There was no remedy for the pain she was in. "Did you have tea at the Parker Hotel on Friday?"

"I met a donor, Mrs. Vandermeer. She wasn't feeling well, so I gave her some of my tea. She said it made her feel better." Amber was wringing her hands.

"Room 817?" Jessica sat on the stool beside her. *Why is she so nervous? What's she hiding?*

"How'd you know that?" Amber's eyes widened.

"That's where Nick's body was found."

Amber screwed up her face. "How's that possible? That was Mrs. Vandermeer's room. Did Nick visit Mrs. Vandermeer?"

"Tell me about this Mrs. Vandermeer." Jessica studied her friend, looking for tells.

"She's a rich lady who wants to donate to the new Center for Russian Art. I brought her the paperwork and gave her some tea. That's all I know." Amber was fidgeting on her stool.

"What did she look like?" Jessica wasn't in the mood to be gentle. She was going to get to the bottom of Nick's death, even if it meant alienating Amber. *Even if it means sending her to prison?*

"She's tall and very pretty with ash silver hair done

up like one of those old film stars, not like the other old ladies I meet." Amber fluttered her hands in front of her face as she took another bite of toast. "A beautiful dye job. Must have cost her a fortune. Unless it was a wig... and still cost her a fortune."

"How was she different?" Jessica rubbed her temples. Her head ached. She needed caffeine.

"Her face was so young. She could pass for thirty." Amber took a sip of tea. "Most older rich women have had so much plastic surgery they look like the Joker."

"What's Mrs. Vandermeer's first name?"

"I don't know. I guess it was on the paperwork. I don't remember." Amber rubbed her hands together like she was cold.

"What about Nick's dad? Why didn't you tell me you met him for tea?" Jessica narrowed her eyes, watching her friend closely. Sucking on the end of her snaky hair was Amber's tell. Why would she be protecting this Mrs. Vandermeer? Something about this whole thing stunk worse than a cow barn.

Amber coiled a snaky lock around her finger. "I didn't meet him for tea. I met him about his donation to the Center and delivered the documents for him to sign." She flipped tail end into her mouth. "Amira had a stomachache, so I gave her some tea. And Mr. Schilling was anxious, so I offered him some too. Chamomile is a warming and healing herb—"

"Why didn't you tell me about Amira when I asked

you at Pavlov's?" *I knew it!* Amber *had* been hiding something. She was going to get the truth out of her friend if it was the last thing she did. "Who is Amira?"

"One of the refugee girls." Amber giggled—another tell. She was nervous.

"What was she doing with Mr. Schilling?"

"He gave the girls money. He was helping Girls First."

"That explains the clause in the estate pledge that Detective Cormier asked about."

Amber's face turned beet red. "Detective Cormier was asking about a clause in the VIPER agreement?"

"The pledge had a clause about donating to refugees." Jessica chewed on a fingernail. "Nick thought that was weird—"

"I did something I shouldn't have . . ." Amber's voice trailed off.

"Amber, what did you do?" Jessica narrowed her eyes and stared at her friend. But Amber tapped her phone.

"I'm late. I've got to go."

"How about I come with you to the Parker and you tell me on the way?" Jessica stood up.

Amber's lips twitched. She popped a snaky coil into her mouth again. "Um. Okay." She slid off the stool, left again, and reappeared with a large white envelope, which she stuffed into her giant purse.

On the train ride, Jessica grilled Amber until she finally confessed.

"I added the refugee clause to Mr. Schilling's VIPER pledge," Amber said sheepishly.

"You did what?"

Amber chewed a lock of hair, nodding.

"Wow!" Jessica grinned. She couldn't believe her flighty friend had done something so bold. "I'm impressed."

"Promise you won't tell," Amber pleaded.

"Now that Mr. Schilling is dead, do you think the pledge statement still holds? I mean, he wouldn't have the refugee clause in his will or anything." *Is it right to do something wrong if it helps other people? It may be illegal, but is it immoral to want to help refugees?* She struggled to reconcile what was legally right with what was ethically right. As a philosopher, she'd always had a hard time with the moral high ground.

"Those girls really need help." Amber's eyes shone with tears.

"Okay. I suppose it won't hurt anyone to think Mr. Schilling was a philanthropist . . ." Jessica shook her head. All this time, she'd thought Amber had been involved in the murderers. She'd underestimated her friend. By the time the train stopped, Jessica had forgiven Amber for putting her through the last week of worrying hell.

As soon as Jessica stepped into the Parker's

cavernous lobby, an invisible hand reached inside her chest and squeezed. Nick's smile, his cologne, his warm touch—it all came flooding back. She clamped her eyes shut to stop the tears. When she opened them again, she saw Nick at the reception desk. Her mouth fell open. "Nick?" she whispered.

"Are you okay?" Amber led her to the elevator. "Here."

"Who is that man at the reception desk?" Jessica stood paralyzed in disbelief. *Am I seeing ghosts now?* He looked exactly like Nick.

"*What* man?" Amber rummaged in her purse and pulled out another tiny blue vial. "Calm-X. Hold these drops under your tongue for thirty seconds." She held out the dropper.

Jessica closed her eyes and opened her mouth. She held the bitter liquid under her tongue, hoping it would chase away any spirits.

"Darlings!" A familiar voice came from behind them. "What a surprise." Lolita gave them each a hug and cheek kisses. "What are you doing here?"

"We could ask you the same," Jessica said.

"I'm visiting my grandmother. I haven't seen her since she went back to Moscow." Lolita pushed the elevator button. "She's in town for the grand opening of Nick's Center."

"Nick's dead," Jessica blurted out. Her heart seized up. She could hardly breath.

"What?" Lolita put a manicured hand to her mouth. "How?"

"Heart attack from Amber's poisoned tea bags." Jessica glared at Amber.

"That's not true!" Amber's mouth fell open.

Jessica knew she shouldn't accuse her friend, but with so little sleep, she couldn't control what came out of her mouth.

"Let's go to my grandmother's room and sit down. We need a drink." The elevator opened and Lolita held her arm across the door. "After you."

"Can you push seven?" Amber asked.

Jessica pushed seven.

Lolita shot her an odd look. "My grandmother is on the seventh floor."

"So is my donor . . ." Amber pulled the envelope from her purse and removed a sticky note. "I'm meeting a 'Countess Volkov.'"

"My grandmother!"

"Your grandma is a countess?" Amber stuffed the envelope back in her bag.

"After my grandfather died, she married her cousin, Count Volkov. The love of her life." Lolita smiled wistfully. "Her life is better now. It wasn't easy being married to a Bratva boss."

"Wait—so Lolita's grandmother is your donor?" Jessica scowled. "I hope she doesn't end up like the last ones."

Amber wrapped a lock of hair around her finger and gave Jessica a sad puppy dog look.

"Sorry," Jessica said. "I'm not myself today."

"Why don't we all go see grandmother together? She would enjoy seeing you girls, too." Lolita stretched her long arm across the elevator door as they exited on the seventh floor. "And I think we could all use a Bloody Mary or a mimosa. The tension is palpable." Lolita laughed. "Why don't you two kiss and make up?"

The countess's room smelled of lilacs and cinnamon. Countess Volkov was an elegant, commanding woman and an older version of her granddaughter. Her black hair, streaked with gray, was pinned up in a chignon at the back of her graceful neck. She floated around the room in a red satin dressing gown and matching slippers.

"Lolita, darling." She embraced her granddaughter.

Lolita was smiling from ear to ear. "I've missed you so much."

"*Ya lyublyu vas.*" The countess kissed her granddaughter's cheek.

"I love you, too." Lolita took her grandmother's hand and kissed it.

"Girls, come sit," the countess said with a lilting accent, gesturing toward a sofa. "I will order tea."

Jessica winced. "Why don't we have coffee instead?"

"It's too late in the morning for coffee, *milaya*." Volkov waved her long-fingered hand in the same gesture Lolita made when dismissing a rowdy poker player.

"A cocktail, then," Lolita said, heading for the minibar.

"You're so like your grandfather." When the countess smiled, there was a luminescence that made even the ceiling sparkle.

"Which one?" Lolita arched a brow.

The countess threw her head back and laughed.

"You remember Jessica and Amber." Lolita gestured toward her friends.

"Countess Volkov," Amber said, extending her hand. "Sorry to interrupt your reunion, but I work at the development office and, well, have you had time to look over the documents I sent to you?" Her cheeks turned bright red as she bounced up and down on her toes.

"Shall we get the business over with so we can enjoy our tea?" The countess led them to the sitting area, settled in an upholstered chair, and crossed her long legs.

Amber sat next to her and fished the envelope from her purse. "As you know, these are the documents regarding your donation to the Center for Russian Art and Culture. We greatly appreciate your donation." She handed the envelope to the countess. "Let me explain the documents. If you turn to the first page, that's a statement of intent to leave a portion of your estate to the Center upon your death—which, God willing, won't be for a long while—"

"Yes," the countess gave another dismissive wave. "No need to bore us with the details. I will examine them at my leisure."

"Please sign one set and return it in the envelope provided." Amber sounded like a robot delivering a canned spiel.

"Of course." The countess leaned over and laid the envelope on the coffee table. "My son works at the Center for Russian Art. He always wanted to be an artist." She sighed. "Donating to the Center is the least I can do for him."

There was a knock on the door signaling the arrival of room service. The porter rolled in a cart, and the countess discreetly handed him a bill. She had ordered a tea service for four, along with smoked salmon, duck pâté, and an assortment of prim little cookies.

Jessica's stomach growled. She hadn't eaten since yesterday. Without her usual strong morning coffee, her head was pounding. Hopefully, a strong cup of tea and something sweet would take the edge off. The Russians liked their tea strong.

"Grandmother, let me steep the tea." Lolita flipped through the assortment of tea bags and pulled out a handful wrapped in red. She peeled them open.

"Just what I need for the jet lag," the countess said. "A strong cup of tea."

"I have something for jet lag!" Amber pulled a baggie out of her purse. "This tea is a special blend of energizing herbs guaranteed to fight jet lag." She handed the baggie to the countess, who took it cautiously, as if it might bite. "Yerba maté is stimulating without the jitters. Guarana improves mental focus. And Schisandra berry is an adaptogenic energy booster."

"Intriguing. I suppose it can't hurt." The countess held out the baggie to Lolita. "Add a few of these to our teapot, *moya lyubov*."

Jessica shook her head. "I don't think we should . . ."

The idea was so far-fetched. And yet, why had Amber been so secretive about meeting Nick's father? On the train, she'd confessed to adding that clause to the will . . . but was that all she'd done? None of it made sense.

Lolita dropped another wad of tea bags into the pot. "I hope this water is hot enough," she said as she stirred. "It smells . . . interesting."

Dreadful, more like. On top of the sharp smell of strong black tea danced a devilish, earthy fragrance. Jessica wrinkled her sensitive sniffer. Her nose rivaled that of any wild animal. In the woods, she could track elk by their scent. For better or worse—usually worse—her sense of smell was her superpower.

Lolita poured four cups of tea. Tentatively, Jessica sniffed it. The usual lavender-and-clove scent of Amber's energizing blend hit her sinuses.

Still, poison or no poison, Jessica needed something stronger than tea. A bit of the hair of the dog. Lolita was right. She needed a stiff drink.

Here she was, having a tea party in the snooty Parker Hotel, when she should be writing her dissertation—or, at the very least, finding Nick's killer.

Unless the killer's sitting right across from me . . .

15

The moment of truth. Could he carry it off? Dmitry crouched behind a pillar on the Center's second floor, checking his watch. Vanya had been gone nearly ten minutes. If he didn't hurry, the watchman would return from his rounds. He hoped his cousin knew what he was doing. Vanya bragged he could disable any computer surveillance camera. *He'd better make good on that promise, Dmitry thought, or we'll both end up in jail.*

Another hour to go until Sergei showed up, and Dmitry still had to replace the original paintings with his copies—he refused to use the word *forgeries*. Even Mr. Nick couldn't tell the difference at first glance. The grand opening of the Center had been postponed until the board of trustees could hire a new director. But the security guard was still on duty, making his rounds every hour on the half hour, more or less. It was the *more or less* that worried Dmitry.

He peeked around the pillar. The galleries were dimly lit, and you could hear a *shtift* drop. The guard's keys jangled in the distance, and Dmitry jerked himself back behind the pillar. He'd made Vanya trade his slick Italian lace-ups for sneakers. It was going to be tricky replacing the three paintings without making any noise.

The copies were stored in Dmitry's office. Painting them had been time-consuming, but not as difficult as matching the frames. Doubtless, Sergei would cut them out of their frames, but Dmitry had to make them look authentic to avoid his brother's suspicion. There was no way Dmitry would let those priceless Kandinskys out of his sight. Since Sergei was stealing them and selling them on the black market, it would be a long while before someone noticed they weren't authentic. And even if they did, what were they going to do? Report it to the police? If Sergei found out, he'd have Dmitry's head on a Zhostovo tray. Luckily, Sergei knew as much about art as a Siberian wood beetle. Anyway, if Dmitry's plan worked, Sergei would never get the chance.

Dmitry checked his watch again. What was taking Vanya so long? He peeked around the pillar and saw the guard heading back to his station. *Blin!* Vanya was going to blow the whole operation—

"Hey, boss," Vanya whispered from behind.

Dmitry gasped. "Don't sneak up on me!" he hissed. "Well, what happened? Did you do it?"

Vanya flashed his golden grin. "Does the Pope shit in the woods?"

Dmitry smirked. "You're mixing your idioms."

"Are you calling me names, cousin?" Vanya scowled.

Dmitry shook his head. "Come on. We've got to replace the paintings before Sergei arrives."

"Why can't we just give him your fakes when he gets here?" Vanya whispered as they tiptoed back to Dmitry's office. "Seems stupid to hang up the fakes in order to take them down again."

"I agree." It really was absurd that Sergei insisted on joining this "adventure," as he called it—as if felony burglary was akin to ziplining or shooting the rapids. If his crazy brother would have just asked for the paintings, Dmitry could have handed the copies over no problem. Instead, Dmitry had to carry off an elaborate heist and risk going to prison, or worse. The security guard was armed, and no doubt so was Sergei.

"I guess your mom was right. The stupid head doesn't let the feet rest," Vanya said in Russian.

"The devil finds work for idle hands," Dmitry repeated in English. "My mother is always right." After this idiotic caper, he was supposed to meet his mother for dinner at the Parker Hotel. He'd only seen her once since leaving Russia, and that was when his father—or the man he'd thought was his father—died two years ago. At least he'd been able to talk to her on the phone every week. Every time he heard her voice was a revelation—the voice of his childhood, the same voice as his daughter. It was as if his mother had been reborn in Lolita. "The spit image," as Vanya said.

Dmitry gently lifted his copy of Kandinsky's early Fauvist landscape from the office floor. The deep vibrant colors and thick brushstrokes gave the impression of some exotic fleshy fruit. He handed the painting to his cousin. "Careful now."

"This ain't the real one, right?" Vanya asked.

Dmitry shook his head. He picked up his copy of *Painting with White Lines* and admired it. This had been far more difficult to recreate, with its delicate white lines and blurred shades of turquoise and plum. He'd gone days without sleep and poured so much heart into the piece—he hated to part with it. But better to lose this than the original Kandinsky.

To the trained eye, it was easy to distinguish Dmitry's copies from the originals. If he'd had more time, he could have deceived all but the most discriminating scholar. But these copies were good enough to fool any gangster or wannabe collector.

He'd painted the last of the three, Kandinsky's *Composition VII*, so many times that he'd dreamt he was *inside* the painting, meditating in the garden of Eden, trembling on judgment day, drowning in the flood, then being resurrected through color. The painting was so exquisitely detailed that it would have taken him months to copy. Luckily, he'd spent twenty years painting it over and over again—his own private obsession—and had dozens of copies ready to hand.

A painting in each hand, Dmitry tiptoed down the hallway with Vanya close behind. They stopped at the stairs for a breather. Taking the steps one at a time, Dmitry's biceps strained to carry the heavy frames. A noise from the gallery stopped him in his tracks. He turned back to Vanya and grimaced. Vanya shrugged and slipped past him.

"Stop," Dmitry whispered.

His cousin ignored him, descending the stairs at a good clip. When Dmitry caught up, Vanya turned back and smiled. Dmitry gave him the evil eye and continued through the foyer, towards the gallery. Scanning the room as he went, he strained to hear the guard. They would find out soon enough whether Vanya had successfully installed the loop in the surveillance system.

Dmitry carefully leaned the paintings against the wall under the original Kandinsky landscape. He lifted that original off the wall, sat it on the floor, and replaced it with his copy. Vanya watched, then repeated the operation with *Composition VII*. Dmitry tried to lift the original *White Line*, but it was stuck on its hook. He tugged and it eventually broke free, but not without making a scraping noise. Dmitry stood, gripping the frame in both hands, holding his breath. Listening. After a few seconds, he exhaled and hung the copy in its place. He nodded to Vanya, who followed him back through the gallery and up the stairs to his office. They placed the originals in Dmitry's closet for safekeeping.

Stage one had gone off without a hitch. Next came the tricky part: dealing with hotheaded Sergei.

Dmitry waited by the back door. He shook his head. Who burglarized their own museum and stole their own paintings? A brisk knock signaled Sergei's arrival. Dmitry entered the code onto the keypad of the interior lock and opened the door. Dressed in a dark suit, his brother slipped inside soundlessly, like a pro.

Dmitry checked his watch. Ten minutes until rounds. He led Sergei up the back stairs to his office, where Vanya was waiting. Once inside, he shut the door and breathed a sigh of relief. Another hour and the heist would be over, and—if all went according to plan—Sergei would be out of his life. Away from his family.

"I've been curious about where you work." Sergei's raspy voice cut through the silence. "Nice office, Mr. Bigshot."

Dmitry grimaced. *Just another hour*. He thought of one of his mother's favorite sayings: "Trust in God, but steer away from the rocks."

"For a small monthly donation, I can make sure this place is protected," Sergei said.

"Protected from what?" Dmitry asked. "Crooks like you?"

Vanya chuckled and the unlit cigarette fell out of his mouth onto the floor. "Good one, coz." He bent to pick it up.

"No need to be insulting," Sergei said. "Consider my offer. Think of it as extra insurance."

"Whatever you say." Dmitry gritted his teeth. *One more hour.*

"I had a great time with Lolita Friday night." Sergei smirked.

"Stay away from my daughter." Dmitry spat out the words.

"She's going to work for me. Her poker games will make a nice addition to my gambling operations. And I've got some pretty girls—"

"I'm warning you."

"What are you going to do?" Sergei laughed and did a little dance. "Shoot me?"

"If you go near Lolita again, I swear I'll kill you." Dmitry wiped his sweaty palms on his trousers. *Lolita would never work with this scumbag.*

"When it comes to protecting his family, Dima is as dangerous as an Amur tiger." Vanya grinned. "You'd better watch out, Sly."

"Lolita told me Mom is in town." Sergei sat in Dmitry's desk chair. "She's spending my inheritance, donating to your precious Center. All the more reason I deserve something in return."

Dmitry's chest tightened at the mention of his mother.

"Those Kandinsky paintings are rightfully mine, too. That's why you're about to hand them over to me. And when you collect the insurance money, you'll give that to me, too." Sergei put his feet up on the desk. "You and Mom have stolen what's mine, and one way or another, I'm going to get it back."

Dmitry balled up his fists. "Whatever you say." He checked his watch. The guard should have finished his rounds by now. "We've got to move. Timing is everything." *And if I don't time it just right, then I'll be the one caught in the trap.* Dmitry opened the office door and glanced down the hallway, then waved to his cousin and brother. "Let's go," he whispered.

The humming of the air conditioner was the only sound in the galleries . . . along with Vanya's breathing and Sergei's leather soles scuffing against the polished floor. Usually, Dmitry found the empty museum a consolation, his own private place of wonder. Today, the deserted foyer was haunted by childhood ghosts. The stillness reminded him of the abandoned hospital. Dmitry had never had the stomach for killing, but it seemed every one of his relatives did—even his darling Lolita. It was the Yudkovich blood. *Why can't she be more like Sabina?*

Dmitry inhaled the new construction smell, a mixture of shaved wood and varnish, with an undercurrent of Vanya's Old Spice cologne. At least his cousin had his back, right?

They'd made it through the foyer and the Goncharova gallery, which always reminded Dmitry of his mother. For reasons he'd never understood, she adored the blocky figures in *Picking Apples*. The painting had hung in her bedroom, a place he wasn't allowed to enter. Seeing it now further darkened his mood.

The dimly lit Kandinsky gallery was just up ahead. A creaking sound made Dmitry stop. He held up his hand and listened. It was amazing how many noises a building made. When you truly listened, it was like putting your ear to someone's belly.

Dmitry took a few quick steps and found himself in front of *Composition VII*. He nodded at the painting. Sergei snapped open a switchblade and, with too much glee, cut it from the frame. Dmitry cringed. His heart sped up, and he reminded himself it was only one of his copies and not the original. *Thank God.* It was painful enough watching Sergei deface his painting. He would rather be cut himself than see an original Kandinsky destroyed.

Sergei handed the painting to Vanya, who rolled up the canvas and slid it into one of the cardboard canisters carried in the big cloth bag slung over his shoulder. They moved on to the landscape next. The canvas made a ripping sound as Sergei tore at it with his knife. Dmitry shuddered.

"Shhh." Dmitry put a finger to his lips.

Sergei stopped halfway around the frame and stood frozen, waiting to see if the guard had heard him.

A couple seconds passed. Nothing. He continued sawing at the canvas until the painting fell free of the frame. He handed it to Vanya, who quietly rolled it and stored it in a second canister.

White Lines put up a fight, and when Sergei tore the canvas, prying it from the frame, it was as if he'd ripped Dmitry's own flesh.

"Be careful," Dmitry whispered.

Sergei just shrugged and handed the mangled painting to Vanya. But instead of leaving the gallery as planned, Sergei crossed to the opposite wall. He pointed his blade at Kandinsky's *Yellow-Red-Blue*.

Dmitry raced to intercept him. "No!" he stage-whispered as he leapt in front of the painting, blocking the knife. "You got what you came for."

"Why stop now, brother?"

"You agreed to three Kandinskys. That's enough."

"There's never enough."

"Remember, Brother," Dmitry said. "Little pigs get fat. Big hogs get slaughtered."

"I'm not a farmer—I'm the new boss of one Chicago's biggest crime syndicates," Sergei hissed. "And I have an order to fill for as many of these ridiculous paintings as I can get my hands on, so get out of my way." He stuck the point of the blade under Dmitry's chin.

Dmitry winced as it punctured his skin. A trickle of warm blood dripped down his neck, but he didn't move. He would have to kill Sergei to stop him. Either that or change his name again and take his whole family on the run.

Dmitry was tired of running. It was time to face his past head-on.

“Come on, man,” Vanya said. “Let’s blow this bitch before we get busted.”

Dmitry grabbed his brother’s wrist and tried to push the blade away from his throat. “You need me to enter the code for the backdoor.”

Sergei lowered the knife.

“Vanya’s right. We’ve got to get out of here.” Dmitry held up his arms and took two steps away from the painting. “The guard will be making his next rounds soon.” He took another two steps.

Sergei lunged—plunging his knife into the corner of the canvas.

“No!” Dmitry shouted. His voice echoed off the high ceilings and returned to him as if from the far side of the gallery. He threw his arms around his brother’s waist and yanked him backwards. A stabbing pain shot through Dmitry’s thigh and he released his grip on his brother. His hands flew to his injured leg.

Sergei pulled the blade from Dmitry’s leg, wiped it off on a handkerchief, and turned back to the painting. Blood dripped from Dmitry’s hands. It ran down his leg. Still, Dmitry spun his brother around and punched him in the face. Sergei kneed him in the groin, then sent him crashing to the floor with an uppercut to the chin.

Writhing on the floor, nauseated from the pain, Dmitry watched helplessly as Sergei cut Kandinsky’s masterpiece from its frame. He stared up at the red-ringed black dot in its yellow face and thought of Kandinsky’s words:

The sun melts all of Moscow down to a single spot that, like a mad tuba, starts all of the heart and all of the soul vibrating . . . the final chord of a symphony that takes every color to the zenith of life . . .

He staggered to his feet, determined to save the art that gave meaning to his life.

Unarmed, Dmitry didn't stand a chance against his brother. He pulled at Vanya's sleeve. "Let's go," he whispered. "If we take the paintings, Sergei will follow."

"Okay, boss." Vanya helped Dmitry out of the gallery, leaving a trail of blood behind.

Dmitry willed himself not to look back. Panic filled his chest as he thought of Sergei attacking more precious art. If only he could get his brother to follow him to the back door, this nightmare would be over.

The sound of a door opening must have catapulted Sergei into action. Blade in one hand and canvas waving in the other, Sergei flew past Dmitry and Vanya. "Give me the bag," he shouted at Vanya.

Vanya held out the bag. As loyal as his cousin was to Dmitry, he was more sacred of Sergei. Dmitry didn't blame him. Sergei pushed his knife-wielding hand through the strap and jostled the bag onto his shoulder. "Move it," he hissed. "I need the code."

Dmitry limped as fast as he could towards the back door.

"Stop right there!" A voice came from behind them. The security guard appeared, gun drawn.

With a quick jerking motion, Sergei threw his knife.

It whizzed past Dmitry's head and lodged in the guard's shoulder. The guard groaned, dropped his gun, and grabbed at the hilt of the knife.

Sergei pulled a pistol from his jacket.

"No!" Dmitry shouted. "No killing."

"You always were afraid of guns." Sergei smirked. "This *blyad* saw us. He has to die."

"Vanya, open the door!" Dmitry shouted. "Three-three-one. Open it now!"

Sergei lifted the pistol and aimed it at the guard.

Vanya darted to the back door and slapped at the keypad. There was a commotion at the door.

Two uniformed officers flew into the hallway. "Freeze!"

Sergei cocked the pistol. Dmitry lunged.

A deafening explosion reverberated through his skull, and the floor swallowed him up in one violent gulp. The sights and sound of the world receded down a dark tunnel and then disappeared.

16

Everything hurt. As the white room came into focus, Dmitry felt warm pressure on his right hand. He pried his eyes open. *Sabina!* What was she doing here? Where was here? When he explored her face, he still saw the beautiful teenager he'd fallen for in drawing class at the Moscow Institute of Art.

"Dad, are you okay?"

He moved his head toward his daughter's voice. She was holding his left hand. At least his wife and daughter were safe . . . unless he was hallucinating.

"What happened?" he asked. He remembered Sergei. An explosion of pain.

"You were shot," Sabina said, with tears welling in her eyes.

"How bad is the damage?" Dmitry winced as he tried to move.

“The doctors say you’re lucky the bullet didn’t hit an organ.” She smiled down at him.

“Yes, but what happened to Sergei?” The room was still coming into focus, along with the memories of last night. “Did the plan work?”

“If you mean the setup last night, then yes, it worked.” Lolita slipped her hand out of his. “How could you set up uncle Sly? He’s your own flesh and blood.”

“He was threatening you. I had to put him away to keep you safe, *kotyonok*.” When Dmitry reached out his arm, cords attached to his veins pulled him back again. *Blin!* He was hooked up to a machine, some kind of IV drip.

“Don’t call me ‘kitten.’ I can take care of myself,” Lolita said, flipping her hair over her shoulder. “And Uncle Sly wouldn’t hurt me. We understand each other. He’s tough outside but a softy inside.”

She must be talking about someone else. There was nothing soft about Sergei.

“Sergei’s a gangster, not a marshmallow.”

Lolita scoffed. “Sometimes I wonder about you, Dad. You and your haunted past. I think your artist’s imagination carries you away.” She sat in the recliner chair next to the bed and crossed her long legs. “You see thugs everywhere.”

“My brother is a criminal. We aren’t safe until he’s locked away.” *Or I kill him,* Dmitry thought.

“There’s a fine line between crime and good business. Uncle Sly and I know how to walk that line." Lolita laid a manicured hand over her knee.

When she smiled, his heart ached. He'd left Moscow in order to protect his family, to leave that life behind. Now his own daughter could talk about the line between crime and business? It made him ill.

"You have a world-class education. What do you need with creeps like Sergei?" He tried to sit up, but he was too dizzy. The sheet slipped down his torso. He shivered. The hospital room was freezing.

"Where's Vanya?"

"He's out getting a Happy Meal." Lolita scoffed. "He's a true American now."

Sabina replaced the sheet and pulled the blanket up around Dmitry's shoulders. "Rest, *lyubov moya*." She turned to scowl at Lolita. "Your father needs rest. Now is not the time to argue." She squeezed his hand. "Don't worry, Sergei is in jail."

"For now." Lolita pulled a file from the back pocket of her leather pants and filed a long red fingernail. "Bratva will get him out."

"Since when do you know about Bratva?" Dmitry pulled his hand away from his wife and sat up. "I've worked my whole life to keep you away from the brotherhood. If you get mixed with the Russian mafia, your life won't be your own. That's why I left Moscow and my family and everything I knew and loved, except you and your mother—to get you away from Bratva."

"Don't blow a gasket, Dad." Lolita uncrossed her

legs and sat forward in the chair. "Relax. I'm not involved with the 'brotherhood.'" She spat the word out with disdain. "Forget the brothers. The future is female." She stood up. "It's too hot in here. I'm going out for some air." She strode out of the room and shut the door.

"Don't be so hard on her," Sabina said. "She's young. She doesn't know about Bratva. She's a good girl."

"That's what I'm afraid of." He fell back against the pillow. "What she doesn't know might kill her. There's no such thing as innocence when it comes to the brotherhood." His stomach soured as he remembered being a little kid and his father laughing when one of his *Vor* gave Dmitry a box to open—it contained the finger of a rival gang member. "And she's right. The police will be lucky to make the charges stick."

"Thanks to you, he was caught red-handed stealing. He won't wriggle out of this one." Sabina stroked his hair. "Rest now, *lyubov moya*. Please."

Her touch was soothing. "I hope he doesn't have any *Vory* loyal enough to come looking for revenge." Dmitry closed his eyes. A month ago, he'd been on top of the world with a new job and a daughter only one semester away from college graduation. Now, his brother had returned from the dead to torment him. His boss, Mr. Nick, was dead. And Lolita . . . was she mixed up with Bratva? He wished he could rip the tubes out of his arm and go take on the lot of them. But he was too exhausted and drugged up to get out of bed and dressed, let alone challenge Bratva.

With Sabina at his side, holding his hand and stroking his hair, he fell into a fitful morphine-induced dream. He was back at the abandoned hospital. Paint was peeling off the concrete walls, and the floor tiles were cracked. Rain seeped in through the roof, forming puddles and making the operating rooms damp and moldy. His father was laughing as he strapped Dmitry into one of the gynecology chairs, took out a long, thin saw, and sawed off both of Dmitry's legs. He woke up in a cold sweat with an uneasy premonition about his mother. "She's not safe," he said, trying to free himself from the bed covers.

"There, there," Sabina cooed. "It's okay. It was just a dream. Go back to sleep."

"Where is she?" The last image he'd seen in his dream was his mother's face, twisted in agony.

"Lolita stepped outside, probably for a nasty cigarette. I'm sure she's fine. Go back to sleep now, *lyubov moya*." She stroked his cheek.

"Mama," he whispered as he fell back into the morphine-induced haze.

He must have fallen asleep, because he woke up to Lolita's voice.

"To what do we owe this honor, Detective Cormier?"

At first Dmitry thought he was dreaming. But when he opened his eyes, the well-dressed detective was standing at the foot of his bed.

"How are you feeling?" Detective Cormier asked.

"My mother taught me not to mention rope in the house of the hangman." Dmitry smiled.

"And you think I'm the hangman?" The detective patted the blanket over Dmitry's foot. "You saved a man's life by taking that bullet. You're a brave man, Mr. Durchenko."

"Just because one fears the wolves is no reason not to go into the woods."

"Dad, cool it with the Russian proverbs." Lolita stood up and offered her chair to the detective.

Detective Cormier shook his head. "I'm afraid, I'm here on business—"

"Is Sergei going to prison?" Dmitry sat up in bed. "Did our plan work?"

"Thanks to your tip-off. I've been watching him since he arrived from New York. From what I hear, he'd overstayed his welcome there and had to move on. Unfortunately for us, he chose Chicago. Hopefully, we can keep him behind bars where he belongs." The detective cleared his throat and glanced over at Sabina and Lolita, who were standing by the side of the bed. "I didn't come about your brother," he said to Dmitry. "I came about your mother."

"My mother?" Dmitry shivered and pulled the blanket up to his armpits. "I was supposed to meet her last night for dinner after the museum setup. She's probably wondering what happened."

"I hate this part of the job. No matter how many

times I do it, it never gets easier." The detective adjusted his necktie. "I'm very sorry to have to tell you, but your mother is dead."

"What?" Dmitry stared at the detective.

"That can't be," Lolita said. "I saw her yesterday and she was fine. I don't believe it."

"What happened?" Sabina asked, a worried look on her face. She glanced down at Dmitry and took his hand in both of hers.

"A maid found the countess slumped over the desk in her room at the Parker Hotel. Estimated time of death is between five and seven yesterday evening."

"But she was healthy—" Lolita's accusations turned to sobs.

"We also found cups and tea at the scene. It fits the same pattern as other recent deaths at the hotel, which leads me to believe the tea service is not a coincidence, nor is her death from natural causes."

"Sergei," Dmitry whispered.

"Matricide?" the detective asked.

"Sergei's capable of anything." Dmitry pulled his hand free from Sabina's grasp and covered his face. "Poor mama."

"I'm sorry to bother you at a time like this, but can you tell me if your brother has a motive? Why would he want to kill your mother?"

"He claimed she was keeping his inheritance from him." Dmitry pounded his fists into the bed. "Who knows why Sergei kills? Revenge, money—*fun*—you name it."

"Did your brother have any reason to want to kill Professor Schilling or his father?"

"He wanted three paintings from Mr. Nick's father's collection. Kandinskys." Dmitry shook his head. "I want Sergei tried for murder. He killed my mother—" He broke down sobbing.

Sabina sat on the edge of the bed and leaned in to embrace him. He tugged at the tubes attached to his arm and put his arms around her. Whatever else happened, he had sweet Sabina . . . and their firecracker daughter. He glanced over at Lolita.

"How was she killed?" Lolita asked, with rage in her voice.

"Most likely poisoned, if her death follows the pattern of the others. We're still waiting for the autopsy report on the professor. But Mr. Schilling was given an overdose of digitalis, his heart medicine." The detective put his hands in his pants pockets.

"Poisoned?" Lolita wiped her eyes with the back of her hands.

"We found digitalis in the teacups in Mr. Schilling's suite. We found the same sort of tea bags in the professor's room. We suspect the murderer poisoned the tea bags."

"Amber's tea bags? That's *what Jessica was going on about.* But we all drank her tea." Lolita stared off into space. "No, you won't find poison in the tea bags."

"Amber? You mean that friend of Jessica's I met during the date rape scandal on campus?" The detective removed a small notepad from his inside pocket. "What is her last name?"

"Bush. Amber Bush." Lolita gave the detective a quizzical look. "You can't think airhead Amber had anything to do with this?"

"I aim to find out." He wrote on his pad. "What time did you leave your grandmother yesterday?"

"Around noon, more or less." Lolita took a tissue from the night table and dabbed at her eyes.

"You saw mother yesterday?" Dmitry asked. "Why didn't you tell me?"

"She invited me to her room for tea. Amber and Jessica were there too. Amber gave her documents for a donation to the Center for Russian Art upon her death—"

"Convenient," the detective interrupted. "Mr. Schilling had also just signed an estate plan leaving art and money to the Center. He died right after. Who would benefit from these deaths? Besides the Center for Russian Art, obviously."

"Mr. Nick," Dmitry said. "The Center was his baby. But he's also dead."

"Nick Schilling stood to gain, but he couldn't have poisoned your mother and he wouldn't have poisoned himself." Detective Cormier scratched his chin with the pencil. "Unless he arranged the murders in advance and someone else carried them out."

"You mean Nick planned to poison the donors but someone got to him first?" Lolita asked.

"If he had an accomplice, it's possible he could have set everything in motion and then been killed before he saw his plans come to fruition. We're still waiting for the coroner's report on his death. In the meantime, who else would benefit by these donations to the Center?"

"I suppose I would," Dmitry said. "Mr. Nick promised I'd be promoted if the Center did well. He was going to make me head curator."

"Right, but now he's dead." The detective made another note. "Anyone else connected with the Center who might personally benefit from these donations?"

"The trustees?" Dmitry tried to remember their names. "Maybe one of them had a way to turn donations into personal gain?"

"I'll check out the trustees."

"Why would someone kill Grandmother?" Lolita asked.

"It just doesn't make sense," Sabina said to Dmitry. "Your mother was a gentle soul. Everyone loved her." She reached down for her purse and pulled out a small embroidered handkerchief that had belonged to the countess.

Detective Cormier turned to Lolita. "You're named after your grandmother?"

She nodded.

"I'm sorry for your loss. If anyone thinks of anything, anything at all that might be relevant and help us find her killer, please call me. Night or day." He reached into his pocket, pulled out a business card, and sat it on the bed table.

Sabina's tears had turned to sobs. Dmitry took her hand in his and fought to maintain his composure.

"I'm going to find whoever did this," Lolita said, "and make them pay."

"Please don't." The detective put his hand on Lolita's shoulder, but she shook him off. "Miss Durchenko, please leave this matter to the police. You can't take matters into your own hands. It will only make things worse. And it will be very dangerous for you."

"Why is everyone worried about me?" Lolita threw on her leather jacket. "I can take care of myself. And I have access to places your men can't go." She grabbed her motorcycle helmet from the chair. "I'll find whoever did this, and when I do . . ." She shook her hair out, put on the helmet, and buckled it under her chin.

"Please, *kotyonok*, be careful." Dmitry's voice broke. "I can't bear to lose you, too."

"Don't worry, Dad." She bent over and kissed him on the forehead. "You taught me everything I know."

"That's what I'm worried about." He gave her a weak smile.

17

Eyes glazed over, Amber sat at her desk in the development office, sipping Morning Thunder even though it was afternoon. Although the outer waiting room was furnished with leather chairs and fancy lamps, her desk was in a cubbyhole partitioned off from other little cubbies with flimsy walls. Everything in the entrance to the development office was very posh to make the rich donors feel confident, but behind the scenes, the poor staff ruined their eyesight staring into screens and their backs sitting in crummy office chairs.

She opened her textbook and tried to concentrate. Was she really a suspect in a murder? She knew her tea bags didn't kill anyone. But then why were two people dead after drinking her tea? How did her tea bags get into Nick's hotel room? She hadn't given him tea. And now Jessica was mad at her. She had to shake these worrying thoughts and study. She had a trigonometry test later.

Between meeting Mrs. Vandermeer and Lolita's grandma, she hadn't had time to study. It was always so stressful meeting donors and being polite and not messing up—it took a toll. And now she was juggling a murder investigation on top of it all. She slid her purse out from under her desk and rummaged for the familiar vial of Rescue Remedy and a dark chocolate bar.

The vial was cool and sleek. She held the blue glass up to the light in admiration. She had a whole collection of tiny blue bottles filled with healing potions. She unscrewed the stopper, squeezed the little black bulb at the end, and dropped the flowery essence under her tongue. Within a few minutes, she'd feel better. She tapped on her head to realign her chi.

Along with the donors, her weekend had been eaten up by Gary's Young Socialists meeting on Saturday. They used to have so much fun playing chess and eating chocolate bars. Now Gary was so serious all the time. She'd tried to throw her heart into the meetings, but they were so boring. Sure, she was for equality and justice, but couldn't you have some fun while redistributing the wealth? Anyway, talk was cheap. *Those Young Socialists should be helping me with Girls First or doing something practical instead of sitting around talking about overthrowing capitalism.*

Amber unwrapped her chocolate bar and snapped

off a square. Munching on it, she thought of Amira's smile when she'd taken the girls out for ice cream on Sunday. It had been the highlight of her weekend. Seeing those poor girls smile always brightened her mood. She wished she could work full-time at Girls First instead of the stupid development office. She thought of Richard Schilling's estate plan and wondered if the refugee clause would hold. Her knee bounced up and down so hard it hit the underside of the desk.

With her boss out on maternity leave, Amber was the only one in the office during lunch. At least it was quiet—except for the annoying buzz of the overhead lights, disrupting her chi. She got up and flipped them off. When she returned to her desk, she twisted the switches on her gamma meditation desk lamp and her Himalayan salt lamp. Much better. She lit a stick of Satya Nag Champa incense and stuck it into the soil of the African violet on her desk. For lunch, she'd brought a peanut-butter-and-banana sandwich on gluten-free bread, and a baggie full of vegan chocolate chips. Chocolate was an antioxidant, and bananas were brain food. And peanut butter was just yummy.

She put in her headphones to listen to the playlist Gary had made for her. She liked his taste in music better than his taste in politics. She settled in, trying to forget about murders and exams. She had to relax. She took several deep breaths. The atonal melodies and driving rhythms helped. She ate her sandwich. Pretty soon, she was bopping along to the music and munching her lunch, and she didn't notice the well-dressed man enter the room. She gasped when she saw him standing on the other side of her desk.

"Miss Bush?" He extended a smooth brown hand. "Sorry to interrupt your lunch, but I need to ask you some questions."

"You're Jessica's friend, the police detective."

"I suppose you could call us friends. I'm Detective Harvey Cormier of the Chicago Police Department."

She took his hand. "Good to meet you, Detective."

"We met a couple of years ago . . . when Professor Schmutzig was murdered by his student." Detective Cormier pointed at a wooden chair. "May I?"

She nodded.

Detective Cormier took a seat. "We found these tea bags in Countess Lolita Volkov's hotel room." He held out a zip-lock bag containing Amber's homemade linen tea sachets.

"My energizing blend . . . but why do you have them?" Her pulse quickened.

"The countess is dead."

Amber's stomach did a flip, and she reached for the trash can. *Impossible*, she thought, *I just saw her. No, no, no. It wasn't my tea.*

"Mr. Richard Schilling and his son, Nick, were also murdered. And, not coincidently, your homemade tea bags were found at the scene in each case. In the case of Richard Schilling, we found digitalis in his teacup."

"What is digitalis?" Her voice shook.

"Heart medicine. Too much causes a heart attack."

She shifted in her chair. "I don't use any medicines in my tea. Only organic herbs." Her palms were sweating. "I gave Mr. Schilling my chamomile-lavender blend to help with his anxiety, and I gave the Countess energizing tea to help with her jetlag."

"What made you think Mr. Schilling was anxious?" Detective Cormier took a pen from his vest pocket and clicked it.

"He was pacing the room and seemed very impatient, like he wanted me to leave. He was waiting for his wife." She twirled a lock of hair around her finger.

"Why do you say that?" Detective Cormier wrote something in a small black leather notebook.

"He got a phone call and called the person on the other end 'Honey.' And he said 'see you soon' before he hung up. He said he was waiting for his wife . . . but maybe it was a girlfriend?" She flipped the end of her hair into her mouth. "Amira had a stomachache, so I gave her my Tummy Blend tea."

"Amira?" Detective Cormier glanced up from his notebook.

"Amira is a Syrian refugee. I know her from Girls First, where I volunteer. Last time I met Mr. Schilling, he had a different teenage girl with him. Lila, another of my refugee girls." She scowled.

"Tell me more about these girls." The detective gave her a stern look.

"Gary thinks Mr. Schilling was a human trafficker who set up rich men with wayward refugee girls." She giggled. She didn't mean to, but she couldn't help it. When she got nervous, she giggled. She didn't mention Gary's sister, Julie. "But Mr. Schilling was just trying to help them . . . Those girls have it so rough. They're desperate."

"Who's Gary?"

"My boyfriend. Gary Calloway."

Detective Cormier scowled. "Human trafficking is serious business. Tell me more about your refugee girls."

"I volunteer at Girls First. It's an organization that helps refugee girls and young women. I don't know how, but Mr. Schilling knew some of them. They'd disappear for a few days, then come back wearing gold jewelry or new designer shoes."

"I'll look into that." Detective Cormier nodded. "What about Countess Volkov? Did you give her the same tea?"

"No. I told you, she was suffering from jetlag. So I gave her my Energy Boost blend." *He doesn't really suspect me of murder, does he?* She reached for the vial of Rescue Remedy on her desk.

"And what about the professor? What kind of tea did you give him?" Detective Cormier stared at her, his pen ready.

"You mean Nick? I didn't give him any tea."

"You didn't have tea with Nick Schilling last Friday?"

Detective Cormier tapped his pen against his notebook.

"No. I didn't. He wasn't a donor. I'm sent out to deliver documents to donors. Sometimes I offer them tea." She wrapped a lock of hair around her finger. "I was just trying to help—"

"What about Mrs. Schilling? Did you have tea with her?"

"Mrs. Schilling? Nick is married?" She fidgeted in her chair. "Poor Jessica—"

"No. *Richard* Schilling's wife, Chrissy."

"Oh." Amber discretely lifted the blue vial from her desk and dropped some more Rescue Remedy under her tongue.

A knock on the partition startled her. Before she could say "Come in," Jessica appeared in the entryway. She looked like a hipster model in her vintage sundress and red cowboy boots.

"Speak of the devil," Amber said. "We were just talking about you and Nick."

JESSICA BLEW AT HER BANGS. *Crapulence!* Cormier had beaten her to Amber. He must have finally found out the tea bags were hers. "I'm trying not to think about Nick." She felt a now-familiar stabbing at her heart whenever someone mentioned him. She still couldn't believe he was gone. "Am I interrupting?"

"Join us." The detective pointed at a wooden chair.

She pulled it over to the desk and sat down. "Detective Cormier, good to see you." As much as she liked the detective, it was a lie. Trouble followed him . . . or he followed trouble. *He must be interrogating Amber.*

"Likewise, Miss James." He nodded. "I was just asking Miss Bush about Chrissy Schilling, Richard Schilling's wife."

"That's who Nick was going to meet the night he . . ."

"It's strange. We found digitalis in one of the teacups in Mr. Schilling's suite, and he had elevated levels of the drug in his blood. But now the coroner thinks there's a different cause of death. The amount of digitalis in his system could have made him sick, but it shouldn't have been fatal, since he was taking digitalis for his heart anyway. The coroner is continuing his tests."

"So, could it be a heart attack or some other natural cause?" Jessica twisted the fringe on her jacket.

"I'm not at liberty to give you all the details, but it doesn't seem likely." He glanced at Amber. "The coroner thinks Nick Schilling *was* killed with an overdose of digitalis, and we found the drug in both teacups in the room, which is odd if the perpetrator was also drinking from one of them. He or she would have risked poisoning themselves."

Jessica raised one eyebrow. "Unless the poison was added after they had tea."

"We know Nick ingested an overdose of digitalis somehow. And since his heart was healthy, it didn't take much to kill him."

Jessica grimaced.

"He also had been drinking alcohol. The coroner found traces of juniper, which means he was drinking gin . . . martinis perhaps?"

"We had martinis that afternoon, but vodka, not gin. Nick didn't like gin." Jessica blew at her bangs.

"There was no trace of digitalis or any other drug or poison in the tea bags found in Chrissy's purse or in the teacups in Countess Volkov's hotel room." The detective tapped his pen on his notebook.

"That's because my teabags aren't poisonous," Amber chimed in.

"Who is Countess Volkov?" Jessica asked. The name sounded familiar.

"Dmitry Durchenko's mother." Cormier shifted in his chair. "Lolita's grandmother."

"What? What happened? We just had tea with her yesterday." Jessica glanced from the detective to her friend. *Poor Lolita. She must be heartbroken.* Jessica fought back tears of her own. *So much death, and why?*

"Was the Countess a donor to the Center for Russian Art and Culture?" the detective asked, his pen hovering over his notepad.

"Yes. She was a VIPER." Amber opened her desk drawer and pulled out a silver square. She pushed out two white tablets and popped them into her mouth. "A VIP Estate Retirement donor. But I don't know why they call it *retirement*, since the donation only kicks in after they die."

"It seems someone is killing these VIPERS as soon as they sign the documents leaving their estates to the Center. What's your relation to the Center, Miss Bush?" The detective sat on the edge of his seat, ready to pounce.

"Me? I don't have any relation to the Center. I've never even been there. I just work at the development office part-time while I finish my computer science degree. All I do is deliver the documents or pick them up. And then only because my boss is on maternity leave. I didn't do anything wrong. I just gave away some healing herbs." Her top lip was quivering. She twisted her hair around her finger in a frenzy.

"What do you have to gain from these deaths?" The detective asked, almost to himself.

"Me? Nothing. I wouldn't—" She was trembling, her buxom chest heaving under her paisley dress.

Jessica stood up, went around the desk, and put her arm around her friend. "I know you wouldn't." She glared at the detective. "Don't cry, sweetie."

"You've got to convince them I didn't do it," she bawled.

"Don't worry. I'll find out who did." Jessica gritted her teeth. She'd sworn she'd find out who killed Nick. Now, she had to find the killer for Lolita's sake and to save Amber.

"Did you have tea with Chrissy Schilling?" Detective Cormier asked.

"No," Amber sniffled. "I've never met her. Why?"

"She was in town last week." He closed his notebook and leaned forward. "Yesterday, she was found dead in her New York apartment. Along with a missing royal solitaire diamond worth a fortune, she had these in her purse." He held up a baggie. It was full of Amber's tea bags.

18

Happy hour at Pavlov's Banquet was a game of Russian roulette. You never knew what you would get—recent immigrants kicking back after working construction; Chicago's Ukrainian elite wheeling and dealing; frat boys eating half-price blini and downing vodka shots; or tourists who would never get closer to Russia than Little Odessa in Skokie, Illinois.

Jessica sipped her Jack & Coke at the bar, watching an old couple on the postage stamp sized dance floor, slow dancing to Russian folksongs. Although the restaurant was nearly deserted at five o'clock on a Monday, the smell of cigars lingered from the weekend's checkers tournament. Sometimes she and Lolita would come just to watch the old men play, cuss, and smoke. Usually, it cheered Jessica up. Today, weighed down by Nick's death and Amber's tea bags, a couple old men playing checkers looked like they were biding their time until the Grim Reaper beat them in the ultimate game. *Maybe some food will cheer me up.*

Since Lolita wasn't there yet to make fun of her, she'd ordered her favorite Matryoshka eggs. They were decorated as Russian nesting dolls and stuffed with spicy pickled cucumber—so much better than Lolita's favorite, pork fat. Jessica bit the face off one egg and followed it with a vodka shot. The creamy yolk and tangy frozen vodka fought for dominance as they slid down her throat.

Nick was dead. Lolita's grandmother was dead. Now Chrissy Schilling was dead. Jessica had been sure Chrissy was the murderer. After all, she'd had the most to gain from Mr. Schilling's death and Nick's death. *Odd that Mr. Schilling and Nick had digitalis in their blood, but the Countess and Chrissy didn't. Maybe there are two killers, not just one.* And Amber wasn't helping. She was still hiding something. Jessica rolled an egg around on her plate.

"I see you're behaving like a little school girl again with your decorated eggs." Lolita kissed her cheek.

"If Russian school girls drink frozen vodka shots." Jessica patted the barstool next to her. "I'm so sorry about your grandmother. How are you doing?"

When Lolita closed her eyes, her long fake lashes fluttered like two black butterflies. "Not very well."

Silent tears rolled down Lolita's cheeks. Jessica had never seen her cry before. *What do you say to someone who has just lost a loved one?* Was that something people learned with age and experience? She'd encountered too much death in her twenty-three years, and she'd never learned to cope with it gracefully. She took one of Lolita's hand in both of hers. There was nothing she could say to comfort her friend. She knew that because nothing anyone could say to her would make the pain of losing Nick go away.

"We'll find whoever did it," Jessica said as she squeezed her friend's hand. "We'll find the bastard and make him pay."

"Or the bitch," Lolita said. She waved at Vanya, who was bartending.

He flashed his gilded grin. "Coz. What can I get ya?"

"Frozen Stoli shots, and keep them coming." Lolita tapped a long red fingernail on the bar. "Line them up."

"So sad about Granny," he said. "She was nice to me when I was kid. You know, you are her spit image. Looking exactly like her when she was young." He took four shot glasses and a bottle of Stoli out of the freezer. "Frozen shots. I'll fix you up." He lined the glasses in front of Lolita and poured vodka into each, one after another without stopping. "Shots on the mouse."

"On the mouse?" Jessica asked, hoping mouse wasn't another disgusting Russian delicacy.

"It's on the *house*, not *mouse*," Lolita corrected him, then downed two shots in a row.

He laughed. "I knew that," he said, refilling the empty glasses.

Jessica followed suit and drained two of the shot glasses. When Vanya went to refill them, she held her hand out. "I'd better slow down if I want to walk out of here. I can't keep up with the Poker Tsarina."

"How about Billy the Kid?" Lolita downed another shot. "Maybe he can."

Lolita would never let Jessica forget the time she'd dressed up as Billy the Kid for a Halloween party . . . and later passed out at a high-stakes poker game. Billy had been winning, too.

A news banner on the television caught Jessica's eye. "Turn that up!" she called to Vanya.

"A third death at the Parker Hotel has baffled police," the newscaster said. "The first two victims, Mr. Richard Schilling and his son Nicholas, were apparently poisoned with an overdose of digitalis. The third victim, Mrs. Lolita Volkov, was also murdered. Police have not yet released her cause of death. Police also suspect these three murders are linked with a fourth: Richard Schilling's wife, former Victoria's Secret model Chrissy Schilling, was found dead in her Manhattan apartment. The cops are baffled—"

Jessica rolled her eyes. *Everyone is baffled.*

"What's our plan?" Lolita asked, taking another shot.

"I've been thinking." Jessica bit into another egg. "Nick and his dad were both given digitalis. Chrissy and your grandmother were not." She wiped her mouth on a cocktail napkin. "So, if they were poisoned, it was with something else." She waved the napkin for emphasis. "*But* both teacups in Nick's room were laced with digitalis. I suspect the perpetrator laced the cups to throw us off their trail. The digitalis was actually slipped into Nick's cocktail. The tea bags are a red herring."

"So, do we have one killer or multiple killers?"

"Good question.

Lolita waved for Vanya and tapped her nail on the bar. Jessica twisted the fringe on her jacket. The worn leather was reassuring.

"What about our friend, Amber?" Lolita took a shot and slammed her empty glass onto the bar. "And her poisonous tea bags?"

"We both know Amber is not a killer." Jessica licked egg filling off her fingers.

Lolita waved for Vanya to bring her another shot.

"But the only thing these murders have in common is Amber's ridiculous teabags."

"Okay, I admit, the teabags were at the scene of every murder. But doesn't that seem a bit too convenient?"

"Not if they're the murder weapon." Lolita picked at the red polish on her thumbnail.

"I wonder . . ." Jessica brushed her bangs out of her face. She really needed a haircut.

"Well, what else do the murders have in common?" Lolita stacked the empty shot glasses.

"All the victims, except for Nick, were donors to the Center for Russian Art. And Nick was executive director." Jessica finished the last watery remains of her Jack & Coke. "So, the murders have something to do with the Center."

"The victims were all wealthy patrons of Russian art," Lolita said thoughtfully.

"Your father works at the Center." Jessica swiveled the barstool to face her friend. "Maybe he knows something."

"My father is in the hospital." Lolita's lips twitched.

"What? Why? Was he poisoned too?"

"No. He was shot."

"Oh my God. Is he okay?" Jessica worried the fringe on her jacket.

"He will be."

"What happened? Who shot him?"

"My Uncle Sly during a robbery at the Center." Lolita rolled her eyes.

"The Center was robbed?" Jessica couldn't believe what she was hearing. "Did they catch the thieves?"

"Yes. My uncle is in jail. My father set him up." Lolita flipped her long hair over her shoulder. "Not very brotherly, if you ask me."

"You don't know Sly." Vanya's nasal voice came from around the bar.

"And now I'll never get to know him, will I?" Like a cat, Lolita pushed the glasses to the very edge of the bar, waiting to see if they'd fall off.

"You're better off. You have no idea what he did to

your dad." Vanya shook his head. "Grow up, Lolita. This isn't some Mickey Mouse movie."

"Back up. Your *uncle* is the thief?" Jessica's eyes widened.

"So it seems." Lolita gave Vanya the side-eye. "He's in jail, and I'm hosting a big poker game for him next weekend . . . what was supposed to be the first of many."

"Not another poker game!" Jessica sighed. Her friend was pushing it. She'd already been warned by the cops. And now she was tangled up with the mob.

"Highest stakes yet." Lolita smiled. "I'll stake you if you want to play."

"No way." Jessica poked her last egg with a fork and watched it skate around the plate. She didn't want any part in a mobster poker game. A firecracker exploded in her brain. "I wonder if the robbery is related to the murders. Who else works at the Center besides your dad?"

"I don't know. Nick was hiring staff—"

"I know. He offered me a job." Jessica stared at her hands.

"Did you take it?" Lolita swiveled on her stool until their knees were touching. Jessica shook her head. "You should. Then you could get the inside scoop on the Center and snoop around."

Jessica stabbed the egg and bit its head off. "Not a bad idea."

19

Tuesday was the hottest September day on record for Chicago. Jessica should have been at the library, writing—or at least at Blind Faith, staring at a blank computer screen. Instead, she was schlepping her backpack to the biology lab on the other side of campus. Her face was flushed and hot, and her bangs were sticking to her forehead. The air was so heavy it was hard to breathe. She longed for the dry alpine air of Glacier Park and wished she were in Montana, not staring into the brutal noonday Chicago sun.

With this murder investigation, she'd never finish her dissertation or get her degree. And if she got kicked out of the program, she would be unemployed at the end of the semester. She should have jumped at Nick's job offer. She thought of the lock of chestnut hair always falling onto his forehead, and her breath caught.

Why did he have to come back into her life, so beautiful and loving, and then be taken from her forever? It was so unfair. Everyone she loved was ripped from her life —her father, her cousin, and now Nick. She thought of Jack sitting in a prison cell. At least he'd be out soon . . . and then what? Could their friendship survive that kiss?

She picked up her pace to escape the heat. The air was still, and even the trees looked wilted and tired. The usually gorgeous green quad was turning brown, and the rose garden around the fountain was crispy. As she approached the science and medicine campus, the buildings got bigger, brighter, and newer. Like a stray dog sniffing around the dumpster of some posh restaurant, the humanities always got shorted when it came to resources. Nietzsche said art was the only antidote to the tragedy of life. Judging by the shiny new buildings in the science complex, the administration did not agree.

Jessica sucked in the hot air, desperate for a Coke . . . or even a drink of water. When she pulled on the heavy glass door to the biology building, a blast of air conditioning greeted her. It felt like diving into the cold water of Whitefish Lake in June. She marveled at the high ceilings, elegant curved receptionist's desk, and giant mobile hanging in the foyer. The philosophy department was a dump compared to this. She approached the desk, where a tidy woman sat tapping on a keyboard.

"Is there a soda machine around here?" Jessica panted.

"Around the corner." The receptionist pointed toward a sign for the restrooms.

"Can you direct me to the pain research lab?" She sat her heavy backpack on the desk for a breather.

"Third floor. Do you have an appointment? I don't think that lab is open to the public." The receptionist tapped away. "Would you like me to call up for you?"

She'd hoped to surprise Gary the Geek, but it seemed that wasn't in the cards. "Sure. Can you tell Gary . . ." She scrunched up her face, trying to remember his last name. "Calloway—Gary Calloway—that Amber's friend Jessica is here?"

The receptionist gave her a skeptical look. "Amber's friend Jessica," she repeated.

Jessica nodded.

The receptionist picked up the telephone receiver and waited. "Gary Calloway has a visitor. Amber's friend Jessica." She examined her short, manicured nails while she waited, then turned to Jessica. "He says to come up to the lab."

"Thanks." Her first stop would be the pop machine and then on to confront the mouse torturer. She thought of Jack, in prison for freeing the mice in Professor Granowski's lab. Three years seemed a stiff penalty even if he'd destroyed years of research. *Poor Jack. And it was all my idea.*

She slid two dollars into the vending machine slot

and pushed *E8* for a plastic bottle of Coke. *Ahhh.* Nothing like that first sip on a hot day, unless it was from a cold can . . . or, better yet, a frozen glass bottle. She'd guzzled half the Coke by the time she reached the third floor, where she followed signs to the Pain Lab at the end of the hallway.

She pushed an intercom button and Gary the Geek appeared on the other side of the glass door. He buzzed her in. The sterile white-countered lab looked like something out of a science fiction movie—*Gattaca*, maybe. Two young men wore green paper suits and face masks. They stuck their gloved hands through holes in a glass box, manipulating something Jessica was sure she didn't want to see.

"What do you guys do in here?" she asked.

Gary pointed to the green guys. "Crick and Watson, as I call them, are working on gene drives." He chuckled.

"What are gene drives?"

"They're like ice-nine in Vonnegut's *Cat's Cradle.*" He gave her a crooked smile. "But instead of freezing all the water they touch, gene drives spread fast and copy themselves as they go. We can use them to genetically modify mosquitos so they don't carry malaria, or wipe out diseases in whole populations, or make humans resistant to pain."

"Wow. Amazing." She sat her backpack on a chair. "Do you work on gene drives, too?" Something about his tone irritated her, and she was raring for a debate.

"I do pain research. I'll show you." He pointed to the bottle in her hand.

She tipped it up and downed the last of her Coke. The last sip left something to be desired. She dropped it into a trashcan outside the lab entrance.

Gary led her across the lab to a large tank full of little black-and-yellow frogs. *So*, she thought, *he's a frog torturer, not a mouse torturer.* "These little guys are deceptive. They look cute, but they're poisonous."

"How does that help you study pain, besides cause a lot of it?"

"They secrete batrachotoxin, a fantastic tool for figuring out how nerves conduct electricity. So, I'm studying the role electrical impulses play in the sensation of pain."

"Interesting." *Not*. Why was Amber in love with this nerd? They seemed so ill-suited for each other—Amber was a Rescue Remedy junkie, and Gary was as boring as a week without electricity. *Maybe they both have their heads in the clouds, just on different planets.*

"Yeah. But that's not why you came to see me." He stared down at his Hush Puppies. "You came about Amber." He glanced up at her with sadness in his eyes.

"Amber's in trouble. Her tea bags have been found at three murder scenes."

"I know." He shook his head. "But she's the gentlest person I know. She wouldn't hurt anyone."

"That's why we have to find out who did it and exonerate Amber." Jessica wiped her sweaty palms on her jeans. "Is there someplace we can talk?" She glanced around the lab.

"We can go into my office." He gestured toward the door. "This way."

Gary the Frog Torturer's office was small and windowless. Even Jessica's shared office in old, creaky Brentano Hall was nicer than this. Her windows were warped and yellowed, but at least she got some natural light. And unlike his shoebox office with its functional furniture, Brentano's antique light fixtures and chipped wooden desks had character.

Gary sat behind the metal desk, and Jessica took a chair on the other side. She felt like a student bugging her professor during office hours. She thought of all the grade-grubbers she'd had to put up with and envied the sciences, where tests were more cut-and-dried.

Gary pulled the chain on a banker's lamp. "You want to flip off the overhead lights? They buzz in A-flat and it drives me bonkers."

She reached around and flipped the light switch.

"The joys of perfect pitch," he said.

She sat her bag on the floor at her feet. "Does it seem like Amber is acting weird to you?"

"It's that job." He got that hangdog look on his face again and stared down at his shoes. With his shaggy brown hair and round, rosy cheeks, he wasn't a bad-looking guy. "I told her not to go to work in the development office. Those rich people are evil. But she thought she could do some good and persuade donors to support worthy causes. I think there are better places to spend your energy than the development office at a posh university if you want to help people."

"Your paycheck comes from this posh university." Jessica's gaze was unflinching. "Does torturing frogs actually help people?"

"I don't *torture* frogs. And, yes, my research will actually help people." He smirked. "You're a fine one to talk —a philosopher. How do you help people?"

"I help people think." She shifted in her chair.

"People can think just fine without your help." He returned her gaze. "Not thinking is much harder to pull off."

"Is your life more important than the life of one of your frog's or those poor mice? Is mine?" She knew she should get back on track and ask about Amber, but she couldn't let this slide. Sure, it was abstract. Maybe it didn't produce anything tangible . . . but without it, life was as empty as a mailbox on Sunday.

"A skin swab from one of my dart frogs might improve quality of life for millions of humans. A few frogs for a few million people? I'd say that's worth it."

"I doubt the frogs would agree."

"I think we have a long way to go in learning how to treat each other before we start worrying about frogs."

"And I think the way we treat frogs says everything about our attitudes toward each other."

"Frogs are people, too?" He chuckled. "That's right. Your friend, Jack, is in prison for his animal-liberating ways. If you folks were as concerned with poor people as you are with stray dogs, the world would be a lot better place."

She had to admit he had a point. There was more empathy for homeless dogs than homeless people. "The two aren't mutually exclusive." She thought of Jack, in prison for freeing those poor tortured animals. A pinging in her chest told her she was looking forward to seeing him . . . maybe even kissing him?

"Perhaps you're right and there are enough resources to go around. Life isn't a zero-sum game. But unless the 1 percent are forced to give up their greedy, corrupt, exploitative ways, they will continue playing one group off another until everyone loses."

"Maybe." Jessica remembered the clause in the documents found in Nick's dad's hotel directing his donation to Russian refugees. She knew Amber worked with refugees. "Do you work with refugees, too?"

"Amber volunteers at Girls First. We both volunteer at Refugees Now. My great-great-grandfather was a refugee from the Irish Potato Famine. He escaped starvation only to die in a mining accident. He was just a teenager."

"Sorry to hear that."

"My grandfather and dad both worked in the mines. My dad died last year. Coal worker's pneumoconiosis—black lung." He tapped a pencil against his desk.

"That's terrible."

"Yes. It was. If I can help others avoid that kind of

pain and suffering . . ." His gaze was intense, and the tapping picked up speed. "I'm going to do everything in my power to help, in the lab and out."

Jessica stared down at her backpack, wondering how her own research helped refugees, or miners, or poor people, or anyone else. Maybe Gary the Frog Torturer was right. Philosophy wasn't going to cure black lung or rescue refugees. Had she done everything in her power to help anyone? *Wait a minute . . .*

"Everything in your power," she repeated.

20

A bit worse for wear, Dmitry was glad to be back at work just three days later, even if he wasn't sure he'd still *have* a job the following week. With Mr. Nick dead and a string of murdered donors under investigation, the Center might be closed for good. But this morning, Dmitry was looking forward to reframing the Kandinskys he'd rescued from Sergei. It would take a while, but he could work the canvas and adjust the frames. He enjoyed working with his hands.

With his brother behind bars, Dmitry's wife and daughter were safe, at least for now. He thought of his poor mother. Why did Sergei do it? He was getting the paintings, or at least he thought he was. Dmitry hoped they locked up Sergei for life.

He picked up Kandinsky's *Composition* and admired it, as he'd done so many times before. The symphony of colors and shapes had gotten him through many tough nights over the last two decades. He gently wiped the frame with his cloth, careful not to touch the canvas. Staring at the painting, Dmitry lost himself in a particular patch of soft green shaded with gold. He thought of childhood summers at the Count's estate, running through the grass, fly-fishing in the stream—those glorious weeks without his tyrannical father. The Count was his mother's cousin, and it had all seemed so innocent. Even his father didn't suspect anything.

His phone buzzed in his pocket, bringing him back from his daydream. Lolita was texting from outside. *What is she doing here?* He slowly sat the painting on the floor, leaned it against the wall, then hurried to open the back door. He winced. *Too fast.* His legs needed time to heal.

He hoped Lolita wasn't in trouble. Yes, she insisted she could take care of herself. But even a black belt in karate was no match for Sergei's MSS VUL . . . or any thug's gun, for that matter. She was young and thought she was invincible, and that just made her more vulnerable.

He entered the code and opened the door. Lolita, her friend, and Vanya were waiting in the back alley.

"What's going on?" Dmitry asked.

"We want to take a look around." Lolita kissed one cheek and then the other. "And ask you some questions." She was getting so thin. She really needed to come home for some of Sabina's *pelmeni*—so much better than Italian tortellini.

Vanya blew out a cloud of smoke. “Hi, boss.” He flashed his toothy grin, dropped his cigarette on the pavement, and ground it out.

“Thanks, Mr. Durchenko,” Jessica said as they filed past. Poor girl had dark circles under her eyes. With her hair going every which way, she looked like she’d just tumbled out of a dryer. *She must be taking Mr. Nick’s death pretty hard.*

He thought of one of his mother’s sayings, “Death doesn’t take the old, but the ripe.” Mr. Nick had been in the prime of his life. In a sense, Dmitry’s mother had been, too. She’d only recently been freed from the yoke of Anton Yudkovich and reunited with the love of her life, Count Volkov. *Poor Mama. If only I could have seen her again.* Had anyone notified the Count of her death? Dmitry should make a phone call.

“We want to look through all of the donor files,” Lolita said, striding past him toward the elevator. “I presume they’re in Nick’s office?”

“Yes, but it’s locked, and the police have—” He hurried to catch up to his daughter.

“No problemo,” Vanya chuckled. He removed a small black case from his pocket and held it up.

“But the police—”

“Do you really trust the police to find the killer?” Lolita jammed her thumb into the elevator button. “Not a chance. Especially if Bratva is involved.”

“Detective Cormier’s not afraid of Bratva,” Jessica said. She slid past Dmitry into the elevator.

"Well, he should be." Lolita poked the button for the second floor.

"I'm not afraid of Bratva," Vanya said, grinning.

"That's because you *are* Bratva." Dmitry scowled. "And don't have the good sense to get out."

"Once you're in, there's no getting out." Vanya slapped him on the shoulder as they all left the elevator. "Right, boss?"

Vanya was right. As hard as Dmitry had tried to escape Bratva, they'd always caught up to him. He couldn't hide all his life. Even staying out of trouble and cleaning up other people's shit for a living hadn't been enough to go undetected by the brotherhood. They had eyes and ears everywhere. Otherwise, how had Vanya found him two years ago?

"Nick's office," Jessica said. Her hand was trembling as she pointed at a glass door.

"This is a very bad idea." Dmitry shook his head. "My job is hanging by a thread as it is."

"Don't be such a worrying wart." Ignoring the yellow police tape, Vanya removed a long, thin steel tool from his pouch and jimmied the lock. When the door clicked open, he glanced over at Dmitry and grinned. "Easy and peasy." Like a runner finishing a race, Vanya strode right through the police tape. The girls followed him into the office.

"What are we looking for?" Vanya spoke around an unlit cigarette.

"Anything related to the donors," Jessica said. "Especially the VIPERS whose donations kick in only after they croak."

"Yeah. Anything that suggests Nick was raising money for his precious Center by offing people." Lolita sat in Nick's chair and opened his desk drawers.

"Nick didn't kill anyone!" Jessica glared at Lolita, then picked up a laptop from the desk. "What about his computer? We need Amber to hack it for us."

"Amber is another prime suspect," Lolita protested.

"She's definitely hiding something." Jessica sat on the windowsill behind the desk, kicked her feet up on the back of Lolita's chair, and balanced the computer on her thighs. "But I don't think she's a killer."

"I still think my brother had something to do with all this." Dmitry stiffened. "And he is a killer."

"Sly always did have good timing," Vanya said.

Dmitry frowned. "Sergei shows up and everything goes to hell. It can't be a coincidence."

"If Bratva's behind this, we're screwed." Lolita was rifling through some papers she'd removed from a manila folder in the bottom drawer. "The only way to get to the brotherhood is from the inside."

JESSICA TRIED to guess the password on Nick's computer. *Is it his initials, or his birthday? His mother's maiden name?* On a whim, she entered her own name. *Nope. Unless . . .* She typed "dolce" into the box on the screen. Nope. She played around with various numbers —his birthday, her birthday, the date they'd met . . . *Bingo!* She was in. The Tinder icon made her wonder if this was such a good idea. She had no right to be jealous. It's not like they were together.

What am I looking for? What would make someone want to kill Nick? Had he known something about his father's business, something that had gotten him killed? She refused to believe he was actually involved with any shady business deals. Scrolling through his e-mail was worse than looking through his underwear drawer. "Sorry, Nick," she said under her breath.

"These accounts don't add up," Lolita said, holding up a ledger. "Why was Nick selling art donated to the Center?"

"He was selling paintings?" Jessica asked. "Don't most museums buy and sell to fine-tune their collections?"

"The Center isn't even open yet and he's sold two major paintings." Lolita pushed the ledger under Jessica nose. "See. And here's a list of paintings he was planning to sell next month."

All Jessica saw were a bunch of meaningless numbers. "Wait!" She grabbed the ledger. "He sold a copy of *The Blue Rider Almanac*?" She shook her head. "I don't believe it. He was more invested in the Blue Riders than me. Oh my God. No way he would sell these."

"Blue Riders?" Vanya asked.

"A group of early twentieth century Russian and

German expressionist artists founded by Wassily Kandinsky," Dmitry said. "Mr. Nick's specialty."

The former janitor knew his art. He was always as much fun to talk to about Russian art as Nick had been, except with Nick there had been the added benefits of a beautiful face and cute butt. If only she could stop thinking about him. She'd blown her nose raw over the last few days. At night, she cried herself to sleep and woke up parched.

She stopped scrolling. "A message from Nick's dad." She opened it and skimmed the text. "Sent three days before his death. He asks to meet Nick and says he has a surprise for him." She swiped to the bottom of the long message. "Then it gets strange, almost as if it's written in code. Has anyone heard of the 'Fersman catalog'?"

"Sounds familiar," Dmitry said.

"The message talks about Bourbons, solitaires, a regent—"

"I remember!" Dmitry came around the desk and peered down at the computer screen. "The Fersman is a catalog of the Romanov jewels, most of which are still missing."

"The Romanov jewels." Vanya whistled through his grill. "Those babies must be worth a fortune." Click. Click. Click. He snapped his lighter open and shut.

"My father—Anton—had a Romanov brooch and a tiara in his safe," Dmitry said. "I wonder if they're still there . . . or if mother . . ." his voice trailed off.

"Reading between the lines, I'd say Mr. Schilling

acquired four pieces of Romanov jewelry and was bringing it to Nick." Jessica looked up into a chorus of stunned faces. "I don't remember Detective Cormier mentioning anything about finding jewelry in Mr. Schilling's hotel room." She bit her lip. "Wait a second. Nick said something to Cormier about rubies and diamonds. This must be what he meant." She thought of Sally What's-Her-Name, dripping with diamonds. Had she somehow gotten the jewels out of Nick's dad, then killed them both?

"I'd say a treasure trove of Romanov jewelry is a motive for murder." Lolita held up a fat file folder. "The file on Richard Schilling's donations to the Center. It's full of sales receipts. Looks more like Mr. Schilling was selling art through the Center rather than donating it."

"Nick mentioned he was worried about his dad using the Center for money laundering." Jessica shut the computer and put it back on the desk. "Could Mr. Schilling's *business associates*—Mr. Teeth and friends—be responsible for the murders?" She paced the length of the office. "I wish we could get ahold of those police reports."

"I got a friend in the police." Vanya leaned back in his chair until its front feet were off the floor, its back touching the wall.

Jessica narrowed her eyes. "Really?"

"What, you don't think I got any friends?" The feet of his chair hit the floor with a thud.

"Let's just say the police seem like they'd be on the

opposite side of the aisle from the brotherhood." Lolita glanced up from the file folder and smiled at her cousin.

"My friend is Bratva. He's vegetable." Vanya chuckled. "How do you think we stay one step ahead of cops?"

"Vegetable?" Jessica asked.

"I think he means *plant*." Lolita laughed.

On Nick's desk, under a pen holder, Jessica spotted a white envelope with her name scrawled across the back. "What's this?" She slid the envelope out and examined it. "It's from the development office, a copy of Mr. Schilling's VIPER agreement." She turned it over in her hands. Seeing her name sent a shiver up her spine. On a whim, she sniffed it—and the acrid smell made her jerk her head back. "What the . . ."

"Excuse me," a familiar aged-whiskey voice said from the doorway.

Jessica got a whiff of citrus and juniper. She gasped. She couldn't believe her eyes. "Nick," she whispered.

"I've come to see Nick's legacy. I'm his cousin, Bobby." He looked just like Nick, maybe a couple of years younger. "Bobby Charis."

Jessica put her hand over her mouth. It was the same man she'd seen at the Parker reception desk just after Nick's death.

"How'd you get in here?" Dmitry asked. He looked surprised. Jessica could tell he saw it too: the uncanny resemblance.

"If this is a bad time . . ." Bobby ran his hand through his hair. "I can come back later."

"That's probably a good idea," Lolita said, a bit too abruptly.

Jessica remained speechless.

"Okay. I'll come back tomorrow." Bobby looked flustered. "Sorry to interrupt." He turned on his heels.

"Wait—" Jessica barely got the word out. But it was too late. He was gone.

DMITRY'S PHONE BUZZED. He didn't recognize the number, but the familiar voice on the other end almost made him drop the phone.

"Sergei. What do you want?" Was his brother calling him from jail?

"I want to see you before I leave," Sergei said.

"You want me to visit you in jail?" That was the only place he wanted to see his brother.

"No. Just come down and open the back door for me."

Dmitry peered out the office window, trying to see into the back alley. "You're here?" His stomach sank. How'd Sergei get out of jail already? Bratva probably owned half the judges in town.

"Uncle Sly is here?" Lolita asked. She sounded excited to see him.

"Vanya, go let him in before he raises a ruckus."

"Sure thing, boss." Vanya lit his cigarette as soon as he stepped foot out of the office.

"Damn! Detective Cormier said he'd make it stick. What's my good-for-nothing brother doing out on the street?" Dmitry stroked his chin. *This is bad, very bad.*

"He probably just posted bail," Lolita said. "I told you Bratva would spring him. They've got the DA in their pocket, so don't count on Uncle going to prison."

"Why don't you take your friend and go get an ice cream or something?" Dmitry took out his wallet to hand his daughter a ten-dollar bill.

"What, and miss the show?" Lolita laughed. "Anyway, I'm twenty-one. I don't eat ice cream, and if I did, I'd buy my own."

"You girls should leave." Dmitry glanced out the window again. A yellow cab was parked next to Vanya's Escalade. "I mean it. It's not safe here."

"That's why we're not leaving, right?" Lolita turned to her friend.

Jessica nodded. She gritted her teeth and prepared for a showdown.

"Last time you saw Uncle Sergei, he shot you." When Lolita flipped her hair over her shoulder, her hand was shaking. "We're your backup." She sounded tough, but he could tell she was scared. "I'm going to make sure nothing happens to you, Dad. I already lost Grandma. I'm not going to lose you, too."

"Please, *kotyonok.*" Dmitry held his hands together in supplication.

Lolita scowled. "You don't have a gun, do you?"

Dmitry shook his head. "Of course not."

"Too bad. Jessica's a crack shot." Lolita sat on the edge of the desk, crossed her leather-clad legs, and picked at one of her red fingernails.

The girl had nerves of steel. The glint in her gray-green eyes reminded him of Anton. He shuddered.

"A family reunion, I see." Sergei barged into the office, with Vanya close on his heels. "I'm glad you're here, Lolita. I need to talk with you."

"Leave her out of it," Dmitry hissed.

"You set me up, Brother." Sergei was standing so close Dmitry could feel his breath on his face. "You won't get away with it." He circled around Dmitry, stopping again directly in front of him, too close for comfort. "You've taken what belongs to me for the last time. So, no, I won't leave her out of it."

"You touch her and I'll kill you," Dmitry said.

"Dad, calm down." Lolita hopped off the desk. "I can take care of myself." She stood in front of Sergei. "I'm not afraid of you."

"I'm glad. No girl should be afraid of her own father." Sergei grinned like a cat stealing cream.

No! Oh God, no! Dmitry should have killed the bastard when he'd had the chance. Sergei was ruining everything, everything Dmitry held dear . . . his daughter, his wife. Why couldn't he just leave them alone?

Lolita squinted, then glanced over at Dmitry. "What?"

"Didn't he tell you?" Sergei pulled off his leather gloves one finger at a time. "Sabina and I, we were lovers before little Dima stole her away from me."

"Dad?" Lolita pleaded.

"I can explain." Dmitry held his hands up.

Lolita's little friend backed into the corner of the office, wrapping her arms around herself. She probably regretted getting in the middle of family business. Dmitry wished he could back away from the scene, too. He felt gutted.

"They probably told everyone you were 'premature,' didn't they?" Sergei bunched his gloves together in one hand and flicked them against the other.

"Dad?" Lolita repeated.

"Don't listen to him," Dmitry hissed. "He's poison."

"Wait. Sly is Lolita's daddy?" Vanya's nervous laughter punctuated the tension in the room. "Whoa. The apple doesn't fall far from the pea."

"Dad?" Lolita whispered. "Please . . ."

He balled his fists. "You're my daughter in every way that matters," he said, finally.

"Except for blood," Sergei said. "Bratva's running through your veins." He smiled at Lolita. "That's why I want you to oversee my Chicago operations until I get back."

"Me?" Lolita asked, indignantly.

"Don't listen to him. He won't be coming back from prison." Dmitry wanted to punch him.

"Not prison, brother." Sergei grinned. "I'm leaving

the country . . . No more tea that tastes like piss or meatloaf that looks like dog food. I'm going back to Moscow. Two weeks in this hellhole is enough for me." He waved his hand as if to diffuse a bad smell. "Lolita will take my place until I'm back."

"You're insane." Dmitry smacked his fist into his palm. "Lolita can't run Bratva."

"Why not? Because she's a woman?" Sergei asked.

"He's gotcha there, boss." Vanya chimed in.

Lolita got a strange look in her eyes. She jumped off the desk and slapped Sergei on the back. "I can do anything a man can do."

"And you'll look better doing it." Vanya winked at her.

"I'm not saying she *can't* do it." Dmitry paced the office. "I'm saying she *won't* do it." He glanced over at his daughter and hoped he was right.

Lolita glanced at him apologetically, then let out a high-pitched laugh. She sounded unhinged. It terrified him.

"It's in her blood and you know it." Sergei slid a chunky ruby ring off his little finger and held it out to Lolita. "Show this to anyone who doubts you."

She hesitated and then took the ring. With a glint of defiance in her eyes, she slid it onto her middle finger.

21

Amber sat cross-legged on a cold slab of a bench. Her breathing exercises weren't helping. The police could have at least let her keep her Rescue Remedy. The waiting room's concrete floor hadn't been swept in weeks, and hairy dust bunnies huddled against the walls. The stainless steel toilet in the ladies' room wasn't all that stainless, and the smell of bodily functions hung thick, even out in the stifling waiting room. A scrawny woman sat beside her, covered in tattoos and moaning like a sick cow.

Amber shut her eyes and imagined she was back in her apartment, sipping chamomile tea in front of her fireplace, instead of this stale-smelling jail cell. She heard sniffling and opened her eyes. A teenager in booty shorts and platform heels was escorted into the room and plunked down on a chair. She smelled like cheap perfume.

"Quit your bawling," the scrawny woman said. "My head is killing me."

"Leave the kid alone." A squat woman in a tight blue satin dress swung her stilettoed feet back and forth. "She's probably never been to the cop shop before. She's a virgin."

"I don't care if she's the Virgin Mary," the scrawny woman said. "I'm trying to sleep."

"Why don't I lead us all in some sun salutations?" Amber piped up.

The teenager glared over at Amber, rivulets of mascara running down her cheeks, and the squat woman laughed.

"Why don't you shove your voodoo shit where the sun don't shine?" The tattooed woman growled.

"My *voodoo* can make your headache go away." Amber scooted over on the bench until she was right next to her. "Put one hand over your heart and the other on your stomach."

When the woman turned to face her and scowled, Amber fell back. The scrawny woman's face was blotchy, and she had a tooth missing.

"I can balance your electrical energy in your body and relieve your headache." Amber held out her hand. "Do you mind if I touch your head?"

"Anything to make this damned headache go away." The woman's bloodshot eyes and beaky nose made her look like a sick bird of prey.

Amber tapped the woman's head and said softly,

"You're stepping into a clearing where the air is fresh and the sun is warm on your skin. Inhale health and happiness . . . exhale disease—"

"Amber Bush." The booming voice startled her. "Please follow me to my office."

Detective Cormier led her down a long hallway. His office was sparse and neat. It smelled of Pine-Sol and onions.

"Have a seat." From the doorway, Detective Cormier gestured to a leather chair. His office was much nicer than the dilapidated waiting room. "I'll get right to the point. Have you ever heard of batrachotoxin?"

"No," Amber lied.

"Neither had I until now." Still standing in the doorway, Detective Cormier wiped his brow with a handkerchief. "It's a rare toxin. Our investigation revealed concentrations were present in the bloodstreams of all victims except Professor Schilling. That's what killed them. Although we did find digitalis in the teacups—and that *is* what killed the professor—we have good reason to believe the poison wasn't administered using your tea bags."

"I *told* you my tea bags were innocent."

"So you did." Detective Cormier gestured toward the hallway. "You're free to go . . . for now."

Amber collected her purse from the front desk, called an Uber, and went home. She stripped off her clothes and jumped in the shower. She needed to wash away the lingering smells of the police station. As the anxiety of the last twenty-four hours melted down the dream, she focused on her breathing. She closed her eyes against the hot water, lifting her face into the stream. She would have liked to stay longer, inhaling the healing steam, but she had to find Gary. *Batrachotoxin.* That was the stuff Gary was researching. *I have to ask him . . .*

She quickly toweled off. Her hairbrush tugged back as she tried to tame her wild curls. *No time to blow-dry.* She fastened her bra and threw on a T-shirt, then her favorite loose overalls. It was a nice change, wearing comfortable clothes—she hated having to dress up for the development office, but those rich ladies wouldn't hand over their money to someone who didn't look "respectable."

Refreshed, Amber called an Uber and headed downstairs. Gary would be at his lab. Why did he even need an apartment? He practically lived on campus, tending to his frogs and computer simulations at all hours of the night and day.

Outside Amber's building, a man in a suit leapt at her. "Miss Bush?"

"Yes?" she said tentatively.

"I'm from the *Chicago Sun-Times*. Can I ask you some questions about the recent deaths at the Parker Hotel?"

"I don't know anything about that." She hurried past him and ran to her waiting Uber, a nearby SUV. She opened the passenger door and jumped inside, landing on a pile of papers. "Drive, please, drive."

She closed her eyes and took several slow, cleansing breaths. What was happening? How had her tranquil life become so full of turmoil? *I should check my horoscope.* Maybe the planets were out of alignment, or the moon was too close to the Earth . . . Something was out of balance. Fighting back tears, she gave her head a tap. She had to find a way to regain her equilibrium. Gary would tell her what to do. Together, they'd figure it out.

THE SCIENCE BUILDING made Amber feel small, just one life-form among so many others. And the lab reminded her of the sci-fi B movies she'd loved as a kid, with their well-meaning scientists and catastrophic creations, giant insects and killer wasps.

One of Gary's friends buzzed her into the lab. She was there so often that everyone knew her. Since she usually brought them homemade cookies or brownies, they were always happy to see her. Today, though, she arrived empty-handed.

"No cookies?" Gary's nerdy friend asked as he opened the door for her.

"Sorry." She shook her head. She didn't want to tell him she'd just gotten out of jail. She glanced around the lab. "Where's Gary?"

“He got a call about a half hour ago and left. Said it was an emergency. Something about his little brother.”

“His little brother?” She reached into the pocket of her overalls, pulled out her Rescue Remedy spray bottle, and pumped a few sprays into her mouth. Gary was very close with his brother. She hoped nothing had happened to him.

“Yeah. I think he might be heading home to West Virginia.”

“Must be bad.” She pumped a few more sprays. “I’d better go.”

As soon as she left the lab, she called Gary. No answer. She shot him a text from the elevator, then bolted out when the doors opened on the ground floor. She needed to catch him before he left town. She raced across campus, and by the time she made it to the main drag, she was sweating. *Perspiring is good detox*. She shifted her weight from foot to foot, waiting for an Uber. She hoped she’d get to his apartment in time.

What if he wasn’t home? Running up the path to his apartment, she wondered if she should follow him to West Virginia. Would he have taken a bus or a plane? He didn’t own a car. Knowing Gary, he just might hitch-hike. *Under other circumstances, a cross-country trip together could be a lot of fun.*

She stood on the stoop, searching in her purse for her key. She pressed the buzzer and continued rummaging. *Why can’t I ever find anything in here?* She heard the keys jangle, but she still couldn't find them. Gary's greeting sounded scratchy through the intercom.

"It's me." She grabbed the door handle and sprinted inside at the buzz.

She climbed the stairs two at a time and let herself into Gary's apartment.

There was a grim expression on his face and a suitcase on the bed. He hardly glanced up from packing as she entered his bedroom.

"Where are you going?" she asked. "What happened?"

"My brother. The mine flooded and he's trapped." He stuffed a wad of socks in the duffle bag. "I'm going to get him out."

"You?" She reached out to touch his arm, but he moved past her toward his closet.

"I know that mine as well as anyone. I went spelunking in all the caves around there as a kid. My dad took me to the mine lots of times." He crammed a shirt into the duffel. "I know a way inside no one else knows about."

"It's too dangerous. I'm sure the mine will get him—"

"The same mine that killed my grandfather and my dad?" He threw a handful of briefs into the suitcase. "I don't think so. I'm not going to let Schilling's mine kill my little brother, too."

She sat on the edge of the bed while he zipped up the bag. "Gary, can I ask you something?"

"Now's not the time to talk about our future." He bent over and kissed her forehead. "I'll be back as soon as I can."

"Can I come with you?" she asked, surprising herself.

He gazed down at her with sad eyes. "You should go to class. And what about Girls First? I'll be okay."

"Detective Cormier discovered my tea bags weren't the cause of death." She fumbled for her spray bottle and took a couple pumps under her tongue. She steeled her nerves. "It was batrachotoxin," she blurted out. "It's a very rare poison."

"Are you sure?" The color drained from his face and he sat next to her on the bed. "It's nearly impossible to get a hold of."

"Isn't that what you study with the dart frogs?"

"That's right. We're close to figuring out how to isolate its numbing properties from its poisonous ones." He smiled weakly. "It will revolutionize pain management."

"Could someone have stolen it from your lab?" She glanced up into his eyes.

"Seems unlikely. Who would do that? Who would even know we're working with batrachotoxin, or that it's poisonous?" He shook his head. "How was it administered?"

"The police haven't figured it out yet. The detective said that until they do, they don't have much chance of finding the murderer."

"I have to go." He put his arm around her shoulders and leaned in to kiss her cheek. "I'll see you when I get back."

She stared down at her hands. She'd been an idiot. How could she ever have suspected Gary? She loved him. She knew him. He was helping people, not hurting them.

"Are you okay? I should have asked. I'm sorry. I'm so distracted . . . my brother . . ."

"I understand." She put her head on his shoulder. "I'll be okay." She didn't want him to go. She had a weird feeling she'd never see him again.

"What were you going to ask me?" He took her hand and kissed it.

She gazed into his eyes and couldn't bring herself to ask. "Nothing." She brushed a lock of wavy hair out of his face. "Be careful, and come back safe and sound."

"I will. I'll miss you, Sweetie." He squeezed her hand and then stood up. "I've got to go or I'll miss my bus."

"The bus will take two days. Why don't you fly? I'll buy the ticket."

"It's only twelve hours by bus. I'll get there tomorrow morning. Even if I flew, I wouldn't get there until late tonight. Not much I could do in the dark anyway." He sighed. "I'd better get going."

She gave him a hug.

"I love you," he whispered in her ear.

"I love you, too."

22

Jessica couldn't believe it. Her best friend had just accepted the Bratva ring, and now she was helping a mobster steal paintings from the Center.

Sergei handed a switchblade to Lolita and told her to cut the Kandinsky paintings out of their frames.

What in the hell is going on? Has Lolita lost her mind? Is she really going to help this lunatic gangster?

"I'll help you take the paintings if you let my father go." Lolita stood pointing the blade at Sergei, like a cat ready to pounce.

Sergei whipped a gun out from under his suit jacket and grabbed Dmitry by the arm. He pointed the gun at Dmitry's head. "Choose. Me and Bratva, or this sorry excuse for a man."

Jessica stared at her friend, half expecting her to kick the gun out of Sergei's hand. She'd seen Lolita do worse with her black belt karate skills. Instead, Lolita winced ever so slightly and headed toward Kandinsky's *Color Study*.

Was Lolita doing it to protect Dmitry? Or, was she actually working with her uncle? Was her uncle really her dad? Jessica's head was spinning.

Holy crap! Jessica wanted to scream and knock the knife out of Lolita's hand. The gangster held his gun to Dmitry's head while Lolita cut the painting free. The sound of the switchblade sawing at the canvas made Jessica want to puke. *Why isn't she kicking the shit out of him?*

Banging at the back door made Jessica jump.

"Open it," Sergei barked.

Vanya took off and reappeared with a uniformed policeman.

Thank God. "Stop them!" Jessica shouted. "That painting—it's precious—"

The policeman drew his gun. "Put your hands in the air."

Sergei dragged his brother by the arm, stopping in front of the last Kandinsky left in the gallery.

"He's got a gun!" She pointed.

"*Hands* in the *air*!" the cop repeated.

WTF? He wasn't talking to Sergei. He was talking to her. She raised her hands above her head. "Aren't you going to stop him?"

When the policeman laughed, his bushy eyebrows wiggled like caterpillars walking across his forehead.

"He's working for me," Sergei laughed. "Like half the cops in the city. Get this one, too." He pointed the gun at Kandinsky's *Several Circles*.

"No!" Jessica couldn't help herself. Watching the defacement of one of Kandinsky's mystical masterpieces was too much to bear. Kandinsky claimed the circle was the portal to the fourth dimension. She wished she could find a fourth dimension to escape this surreal nightmare. "Lolita, why are you doing this?"

Her friend glanced over at her and winked. *What in the hell did that mean? Does she think this is fun?* Lolita had really crossed a line this time.

"Take that mouthy girl upstairs and tie her up," Sergei said to the cop. "Use my brother's office." He slammed his elbow into Dmitry's ribs and the ex-janitor doubled over.

"Sure thing, Sly." The cop grabbed her arm. He smelled of onions and stale beer, and hairs sprouted from his ears. His big paw strangled Jessica's bicep as he hauled her through the gallery toward the staircase. She tried to shake free, but his grasp was too strong.

The smelly cop plunked her down on a chair. He forced her right arm under its wooden arm. He yanked both wrists behind her back. Then he snapped on handcuffs. She gritted her teeth. Her right elbow was bent backwards, and she was afraid her arm would break. She leaned to her right to try to relieve some of the pressure.

"Go on!" Sergei appeared in the doorway, his gun to

the back of Dmitry's head. "*Sit* down before I *knock* you down."

Dmitry stumbled over to the desk chair and fell into it.

"Restrain him," Sergei said.

The policeman stretched Dmitry's arms backwards, around the chair, and cuffed him.

Jessica winced. Without thinking, she'd tried to sit up straight, and her elbow had strained to the breaking point.

"Well looky here." Sergei grinned. "Dima, you sly dog. You had the paintings hidden in here all along." He waved his gun toward the paintings leaning up against the wall. "Lolita, get those, too."

Lolita slid around him and carefully cut Kandinsky's *Composition* out of its frame.

Jessica stared at her best friend, confused. How could Lolita betray her own father like this? *Did I ever really know her at all?*

Dmitry grunted like he'd been hit in the gut. Blood was seeping through his pant leg. The wound in his thigh must have opened up again.

"What did I take before, some of your forgeries?" Sergei rolled up the canvas and stuffed it inside a tube. "Get those other two paintings and let's get out of here." He pointed his gun at his brother. "Those two know too much."

"Sly, hey." Vanya put his hand on Sergei's shoulder. "Not in front of Lolita."

"She's got to toughen up to be Bratva." Sergei cocked the pistol.

"Not cool, boss." Vanya stepped in front of the gun. "If she's really your daughter, don't do this to her, man. Let me do it. You take her and go."

Sergei nodded. He handed his gun to Vanya, then turned to leave with Lolita and the cop.

"Lolita!" Jessica yelled.

At the threshold, Lolita turned back and gave her an apologetic look.

"What the . . ." Jessica glanced over at Dmitry. His temple was bleeding, and one of his eyes was swelling shut. Sergei must have hit him with his gun.

"Are you okay?" she asked.

He nodded. "We've got to get those paintings back and stop Sergei."

"Shhh." Vanya put his finger to his lips. "Squeaky wheel gets goose."

"*Grease*," she said, leaning into the arm of the chair to keep the handcuffs from digging into her wrists.

"Vanya, get us out of here!"

"No can do, Coz." Vanya pointed the gun at the ceiling. "No more peeps out of you two. You're supposed to be dead." He fired two shots, then flashed his gold-plated grin as he left the office.

WITH A MAMMOTH EFFORT and a lot of groaning, Dmitry

dragged his arms up over the back of the chair. He stood, the cuffs still pinning his arms behind him. The pain in his body was nothing compared to the pain in his soul. His beloved Kandinskys were ripped out of their frames and off to God knows where . . . and he didn't even want to think about his daughter. *I spent my life protecting her from Bratva.* Now, he was living his worst nightmare. What was left to live for?

And Sabina! How could he tell his wife her only child had turned to Bratva?

With his hands behind his back, it was hard to operate the telephone. He dropped the receiver on the desk. Looking over his shoulder, he used his index finger to push 9-1-1. He knelt next to the desk.

"Bratva has all the Kandinskys!" he yelled into the phone.

"What?" the operator asked. "Sir, what is your emergency?"

"Send the police to the Center for Russian Art and Culture!" Jessica screamed. "There's been a robbery."

"Yes, a robbery," Dmitry repeated. Such a simple word to describe how his brother had ripped his life apart.

After giving the operator all of the relevant information, he hauled himself to his feet. He had to save Lolita. She didn't know what she was doing. Dmitry forced his legs to move—it felt like walking through water. Blood ran down his leg. And his head hurt from where Sergei hit him. He dragged himself out the door.

"Where are you going?" Jessica yelled after him.

"I'll be back with the police." He glanced back at the poor girl cuffed to the chair, contorted like a pretzel, hair falling into her beet-red face. "Don't worry. They'll be here soon." *I hope.*

Walking down stairs with his hands cuffed behind his back was more difficult than he expected. Off balance, he took small steps until he reached the bottom, then lengthened his stride. Turning the door-knob to the guard's office was also tricky. He swung the door open. The watchman was slumped over his desk. *Blin! Is he dead?*

He moved closer and saw a bloody gash matted into the guard's brown hair. When Dmitry poked his shoulder, he moaned. *Alive—thank God.* Sergei or the cop must have knocked him unconscious.

Dmitry left for the front door. Before he got there, a loud knocking made him quicken his pace.

"Open up. Police!"

Dmitry slammed into the lever to open the door. Two uniformed policemen stood on the front steps. One asked, "Do you have any weapons?"

"No, but—"

Detective Cormier bounded up the front steps. "Mr. Durchenko, are you alright?" Out of breath, he pointed at Dmitry's face. "I heard the call over the radio and came right over. What happened?"

"I'm okay." He'd forgotten his face was bleeding.

"Sergei stole all the Kandinskys. He kidnapped Lolita. You've got to go after him."

"Can you guys put out a BOLO?" the detective asked the officers. "Armed and dangerous."

"Vanya and a policeman are with them," Dmitry said.

"A policeman?"

"A crooked cop."

The detective scowled. "Describe him."

"Tall, dark hair, mustache . . . He had a mole on his upper lip."

"Where's a phone?" Detective Cormier glanced around the lobby. "I need to call this in on a secure landline."

Dmitry turned, waving his hands from behind his back. "Can someone take these off?"

"Can one of you uncuff Mr. Durchenko?"

After a policeman took off the cuffs, Dmitry rubbed his wrists. "Follow me." He led the detective back up the stairs. "The girl is up here, too."

"Girl?"

"Miss Jessica James."

"I should have known she was involved in this."

When they reached the office, Dmitry led Detective Cormier and the policemen inside.

"Get those cuffs off of Ms. James," the detective ordered.

When she was free of the chair, Jessica rubbed her wrists. "Lolita left—"

"My brother took her," Dmitry cut her off. "He's dangerous."

"He has a corrupt cop on the dole," Jessica said, stretching her arms over her head.

"I've got to call this in." Detective Cormier shook his head. "There are too many good men tempted by what organized crime has to offer." He nodded at the officers. "Maybe one of you should go check the rest of the building."

"There's a security guard downstairs. We need to call an ambulance." Dmitry ran his hands through his hair.

Another batch of police personnel arrived and started gathering evidence and fingerprints. After another hour of questions, Detective Cormier put away his notepad. "You two go home and get some rest."

"And my daughter?" Dmitry asked.

"She's a very brave young woman." The detective stood up. "Don't worry. I'll find her."

Dmitry glared. "There's a fine line between bravery and recklessness, and Lolita walks the tightrope."

"She's as nimble as a cat . . . and can be just as fierce, too." Jessica's old suede jacket swallowed her up. She looked like a kid trying on her daddy's clothes.

Jessica's phone buzzed. Still keeping one eye on Detective Cormier, she slipped it out of her pocket and glanced at it. *Crapulence!* A text from Lolita:

Parker Penthouse @ 10. Don't tell ANYONE. **Come as Billy the Kid**

What the heck? Jessica glanced around at Dmitry and Detective Cormier. *What's she up to? And why doesn't she want me to tell anyone?*

23

The hotel clock chimed ten as Jessica stepped out of the revolving door and into the lobby. She felt ridiculous in her Billy the Kid getup. But with Lolita acting so weird, she knew there must be a good reason. Had Lolita really joined Bratva? If so, was this some sort of high-stakes mafia poker game? Jessica shuddered and adjusted her giant silver belt buckle.

Jessica's senses were on high alert. The red-and-gold carpet seemed to vibrate beneath her boots. The fake mustache made her nose itch. But she didn't dare scratch, or she'd ruin her disguise. The short black wig was itchy too. She rubbed her ten-gallon hat back and forth on her head.

Haunted by Nick's death, she didn't care if she never set foot in the Parker Hotel again. But Lolita had always been there for her, and she was obliged to return the favor. Anyway, she wanted to know what the hell was going on. Jessica had known Lolita for four years and never suspected she'd be capable of turning to the dark side. Even though she was closer to Lolita than to anyone, the Russian beauty had always played her cards close to her vest.

As Jessica crossed the lobby, she could smell the damp soil of freshly watered ferns in their pots. A woman's high-pitched laughter pierced her ears as she passed the reception desk. Jessica pulled her jacket closed and strode toward the elevators. She slid her phone out of her pocket and texted Lolita since she didn't have a keycard to the penthouse.

She had just reached the elevators when a man stepped out in a familiar cloud of citrus and juniper. She gasped. It was Bobby Charis. He walked right past her. She began to dash after him, then remembered her disguise. Back at the elevators, she watched him leave the hotel. Her heart sank.

Lolita soon stepped out of the elevator, a broad smile on her bright red lips and a hard glint in her sage-green eyes. Wearing patent leather platform boots, skintight leather pants, and a black bra beneath a sheer white blouse, she looked like she'd stepped out of a *Vogue* special issue on hot biker babes.

"Darling, you came," Lolita purred, air-kissing Jessica's cheeks. "You look great!" She took Jessica by the hand and lead her into the elevator. "Is my dad okay?"

"Yeah. A few cuts and bruises, but he'll be fine."

Jessica could hardly pay attention. She wanted to rip off her fake mustache and wig and run after Bobby Charis.

"Thank God." Lolita exhaled. "Are you okay? You look like you've just seen a ghost."

"I have."

"What do you mean?"

"Never mind." *That guy may look like Nick, but he's not. Forget about him.*

"Let's get you up to the action." With one manicured hand, Lolita waved her keycard in front of the sensor.

"What's going on?" Jessica asked once the elevator door shut.

"A poker game, what else?" Lolita smiled. "I have something for you." She pulled a tiny gun from the back of her pants. "Remember this?" She handed it to Jessica.

Jessica turned the gun over in her hands. "Where'd you get this?" She recognized the stubby 9-millimeter pistol. "Nick's Colt 1911." She felt a twinge in her chest as she remembered wearing his jacket to the police station two years ago and finding the tiny gun hidden in the pocket. She sighed. *Nick, why did you have to die?*

"Nick was a regular at my games." Lolita stepped out of the elevator and into the penthouse. "I didn't tell you because I didn't want to upset you. But after that show-down with Kurt a couple years ago, I started making everyone check their firearms at the door. He forgot to collect it after his last game."

"Lolita, what is going on?" She weighed the gun in her palm.

"No time to explain now. We've got to get back to the game." She gestured toward the living room. "Hold on to the gun. You may need it. Watch out for my uncle."

"Your uncle is here?" Jessica was glad her dad had taught her to shoot.

Lolita led her across the penthouse to the wet bar. "Keep your eyes and ears open. We're taking him down."

Jessica dropped the gun into her pocket and scanned the room. As usual, it was set up for poker. Two large round tables stood in the center of the room. The bar was stocked with top-shelf liquor and fresh carrot juice for that twerpy little actor, Vance Hamm. Next to the bar, on a marble counter, was a fancy spread of hors d'oeuvres: jumbo prawns on ice; prosciutto-and-ricotta wraps; crab phyllo cups; cucumbers and smoked salmon; and crostini with butternut squash, ricotta, and what looked like preserved lemon—the only thing Jessica could eat. She loaded a plate with crostini and then stared out the plate glass window at a chunk of Chicago skyline. To the right, the moon shone off Lake Michigan.

Given the butterflies in her stomach, Jessica was amazed she could eat at all. She was munching on her third crunchy round of loaded toast when she heard a familiar accented voice and whipped around to see Sergei step out of the elevator.

She scooted around the hors d'oeuvres and zipped back to the bar, where Lolita was mixing cocktails for the early birds—some wealthy businessman who owned a chunk of the Golden Mile, and a point guard for the Chicago Bulls. Jessica grabbed her friend by the elbow and whispered, "Why isn't your uncle on some private jet leaving the country?"

Lolita nodded, smiled, and continued pouring expensive booze.

"You're not working for him, are you?"

"Shhh!" the Poker Tsarina whispered, nodding again. She gently pulled her elbow free of Jessica's grip.

When the men had their drinks and had taken their places at each table, Lolita turned around. "Keep your mouth shut and your eyes open."

"What are you up to?" Jessica asked.

"Trust me." Lolita slipped past her and headed toward the tables. Halfway there, she turned back to Jessica and patted her left hip. "No time to explain."

Jessica looked down and instinctively patted her own left hip. *Oh, right—the gun.* Her eyes widened.

Lolita smiled and nodded.

What was her mysterious Russian friend up to now? Jessica put her plate down on the end of the counter, popped one last crostini into her mouth, then high-tailed it over to pick up her chips. She hated the pressure of playing high-stakes poker, but she needed to stick around to find out what was going on . . . plus,

Lolita needed her. *It's the least I can do after all the times she's saved my butt.*

She circled back around the tables and took a seat to the left of Lolita's uncle. By the looks of him, he was an aggressive player, and it was always best to sit to the left of the most aggressive player at the table. If she was really going to do this, she'd better do it right. *Why is Lolita sucking up to this scumbag?* Sergei should have been in jail, not in some poker penthouse. *'Take him down'? How?*

She glanced over at Sergei's crooked cop friend, who was standing guard at the elevator. Something was up. She could feel it in her gut. She tried to get Lolita's attention, but the Tsarina was too busy serving drinks and purring Russian endearments into eager ears. She had them all eating out of the palm of her hand. *These sleazebags are old enough to be her father. Or grandfather.* Jessica would rather starve than go anywhere near the disgusting old creeps. Still, she admired her friend's cold-blooded manipulation of their lust.

In a cloud of jasmine perfume, Lolita appeared at her side and whispered in her ear, "Watch my uncle. I need you as a witness." She laid a cork coaster on the felt-topped table and sat a tall crystal glass on top of it. "Liquid courage."

Jessica took a sip. *Ahhh.* Jack & Coke just the way she liked it, half-and-half with enough sugar and caffeine to boost her concentration—and enough booze to make her forget she was playing poker for ten grand a hand.

She gulped it down like medicine, willing it to kick in before the first deal.

Adrenaline coursing through her veins, she wiped her palms on her jeans and cleared her throat. She hoped Sergei didn't recognize her. Her strategy was to keep her head down and not say anything.

A shiny-faced young man with slicked-back hair appeared from the elevator. He was carrying a hard-sided briefcase. Shifting from foot to foot and moving the case from one hand to the other, the dude couldn't hold still for a second. With a slight bow of his head, he sat the case on the floor next to Sergei. "From Mad Dog. Payment in full." The lackey was wringing his hands. "Want I should count it for you, Sly?"

"No need." Sergei chuckled. "If it's short, Mad Dog will pay later." He patted the young man on the shoulder. "Give my regards to his lovely wife and their new grandson."

"Sure thing, Sly." Beads of sweat dotted his brow. "Mad Dog will let you know if he needs more stuff."

Sergei nodded.

"Anything else I can do for yous, Sly?"

"Only my friends call me Sly." Sergei waved him away. "Now, get out of here."

"Yes, sir." The nervous delivery boy turned on his heels and darted into the elevator.

"Lolita, dearest," Sergei said with a smile. "My buy-in." He pointed at the case.

Had he sold the paintings? Was he using the poker

game to launder the money? Or was it drug money? No doubt it was dirty. Jessica would feel a lot better if she knew the plan.

Lolita took the briefcase to the desk and returned with four stacks of chips neatly arranged on a tray. "Here you are, Uncle. One hundred thousand." One by one, she set the stacks of chips in front of him—black, blue, red, and white.

"I'm sorry I have to leave this town," Sergei said, patting Lolita's hand. "But I know you'll take good care of my poker game while I'm away."

So, Sergei was taking over Lolita's poker game. Jessica detected a steely glint in Lolita's eyes as she smiled and retracted her hand. She couldn't believe the Poker Tsarina would give up her game. Detective Cormier's warnings hadn't stopped her. The Vegas mob's beatdown hadn't stopped her. Why would she give it up now? *What did her uncle have on her?* After the way he'd treated Dmitry, she'd expected Lolita to karate chop his ass, not kowtow to him.

A commotion at the elevator made Jessica swivel around in her chair. Her hand went to her pocket. She wrapped her fingers around the hilt of Nick's gun. The fine hairs on her arms stood up on high alert. *Something isn't right.* Her stomach did a flip-flop, and she wished she hadn't eaten so much.

"Hands in the air," a familiar baritone boomed, and Detective Cormier stepped out of the elevator, gun drawn. Behind him, two uniformed officers drew their guns, too.

In a split second, Sergei had Jessica in a choke hold. "Let me pass, or I break the little cowboy's neck." He spat out the words.

The bad cop pulled his weapon and pointed it at the detective.

Stunned and barely able to breathe, Jessica's hands flew to her throat. She'd dropped the gun, and it had bounced on the carpet. Gasping, she clawed at the arm around her neck. The room was spinning. Her eyes watered. Desperate for air, she scratched at Sergei's face, but he tightened his grip.

Through a blur of tears, she saw a black boot crack against the side of his head. At the same time, a shot exploded into the room. Something splattered the back of her neck as Sergei flew off his chair, taking her with him. She landed on top and scurried under the table before he could grab her again. Her vision was still blurred, but she felt the cold, hard nub of a gun next to her right hand. She snatched it up, not sure what to do next.

Screams. Chairs kicked over. Poker chips flying.

Another shot pierced the air. Lolita collapsed onto the floor. Her face was a mask of terror as she stared straight at Jessica, sputtering blood.

"Lolita!" Jessica scrambled to her knees and crawled toward her friend. A hand tore at her jeans, holding held her ankle in a tight grip. She did a face-plant into the carpet. Like an animal caught in a trap, she snarled and kicked at the hand.

"You. I thought Vanya killed you." The hate in Sergei's voice made her want to vomit.

Twisting her torso and propping up on one elbow, she aimed the gun and fired at the arm holding her. The grip released.

Jessica turned back to her friend in horror. A pool of red encircled Lolita's head and spread across the white carpet. Jessica moved the hair from her face. "Please, God." She held two fingers to Lolita's neck, praying for a pulse. "No, no, no." Weeping, Jessica collapsed next to her best friend's limp body.

24

I *should have killed my blyad brother back in Moscow.* Dmitry stared down at his daughter's motionless body. He wiped the tears from his eyes with his fists. The only thing he'd ever wanted was to keep her safe. He'd failed. He would never forgive himself.

Will Sabina ever forgive me? He glanced over at his wife. Her eyes were swollen and red. She was shivering. He went to her side, removed his jacket, and draped it over her shoulders.

The hospital's intensive care unit was cold and dark. Dawn was breaking, and an orange glow seeped through the window shade. The room was quiet, except for the regular sighs of the ventilator keeping his daughter alive. A machine monitored Lolita's vital signs. The doctor said she had a fifty-fifty chance. Dmitry wasn't a gambling man, but he knew that when it came to life or death, those odds weren't good enough.

There was a soft knock on the door, and then Lolita's friend poked her head in. "May I come in?"

Dmitry nodded. The nurse had said no more than three visitors at once.

Jessica's red boots clicked against the floor tiles as she made her way to Lolita's bedside. "How is she?"

He wanted to scream, "She's been shot through the lung! How do you think she is?" Instead, he whispered, "She's hanging in there."

"She's a fighter." Jessica's voice was hoarse. She stroked Lolita's hand. "She'll pull through." With a nasty purple bruise on her throat, a black eye, and a split lip, the girl looked like she'd been in a bar fight.

Sabina whimpered and held an already-soaked handkerchief to her eyes.

A soft knock on the door woke Lolita. Her eyelids fluttered for the first time since she'd been admitted to the hospital. When she opened her eyes, they held an urgent question.

Sabina gasped and flew to her bedside. "*Moya lyubov*. You're awake."

"You're intubated," Jessica said. "Don't try to talk."

"Sorry to interrupt." Detective Cormier entered the room, removing his hat. "I came to check on Ms. Durchenko." He walked softly toward the bed. "Has she woken up yet?"

"Look," Sabina said, her voice breaking. "Her eyes are open."

The detective gazed down at Lolita. "Good work.

Thanks to you, we have the evidence we need to put Sergei Yudkovich in prison for a very long time—racketeering, drugs, stolen art, attempted murder, kidnapping . . ."

Lolita's lips turned up in a weak smile.

"Lolita was working for you?" Jessica asked.

"Yes." Detective Cormier cleared his throat.

"That's why she didn't tell me what was going on. I wondered." *Even so, Lolita should have said something.*

"The museum robbery wasn't enough. We were afraid he could argue your shooting was accidental." Detective Cormier glanced at Dmitry. "We needed to link him to heroin smuggling and get him on racketeering. With your daughter's help, we succeeded. Thanks to her, we've taken a big step toward eliminating organized crime in Chicago, including several dirty cops." He smiled. "She's a very brave young woman."

"So, she wasn't really working with my brother?"

"No, Mr. Durchenko. She was working for us."

Dmitry slumped into a chair next to the bed. "Thank God."

"In fact, if she's willing, when she recovers, we'd like her to continue infiltrating the Russian mafia. As far as they know, she's still Sergei's appointed successor.

"Hasn't she done enough?" Sabina sobbed.

"Yes, Mrs. Durchenko. She has." Detective Cormier stared down at the hat in his hands. "It's up to her, of course."

A nurse appeared in the doorway, her pink scrubs

covered in puppies. “There are too many visitors. Some of you will have to leave. The patient needs to rest.”

Jessica followed Detective Cormier out into the hallway.

“Amber?” Jessica weaved around the detective to give her friend a hug. “How long have you been standing there? Why didn’t you come in?”

“The nurse wouldn’t let me.” Amber bit her lip. “Is Lolita okay?”

“She will be.” Jessica hoped it was true. She couldn’t bear losing Lolita. It was painful enough to see her beautiful, fierce best friend lying there with a tube in her mouth.

Amber leaned up against the wall, moving both hands back and forth like she was trying to form a ball of air.

“What are you doing?”

“Energy therapy for Lolita.”

Jessica rolled her mind’s eye and turned back to the detective, who was on the phone.

“I’ll come back when Ms. Durchenko is able to speak,” Detective Cormier whispered as he scooted past her. “Ms. James.” He nodded.

LOLITA WAS GESTURING FRANTICALLY with her hands. She pantomimed writing on paper.

A nurse with a pinched face, her hair wrapped in a

severe bun, appeared at the door. “The patient needs rest. She’s getting agitated.”

“She wants to tell us something,” Dmitry said, pointing at his daughter’s wild hands.

“I’ll get a pen and paper, but then you all have to leave.” The nurse reappeared a minute later. She put a pen in Lolita’s hand and held up a clipboard.

Lolita slowly wrote on the paper. When she finished, she held the clipboard out.

UNCLE DID NOT KILL GRANDMOTHER. FIND WHO DID.

25

"Come on, Amber." Jessica grabbed her friend's paisley sleeve and tugged. "Let's go."

"Think healing thoughts," Amber called back to Lolita's room as they left. "Poor Lolita," she said when they were in the elevator.

Jessica fiddled with the fringe on her jacket. "For her sake, and for Nick's, we've got to find the murderer."

"Maybe we should leave it to the police." Amber pulled a square of chocolate from her purse, unwrapped it, and popped it into her mouth.

"Detective Cormier is okay. But we can move faster than the cops. They have to follow the rules. We don't."

"What do you mean?" Amber was rolling the wrapper into a little ball between her thumb and forefinger.

"Let's find a place to sit down and plan our attack."

"Attack?"

"Our strategy for finding the killer." Jessica pushed the elevator button. "Come on. There's a Starbuck across the street."

"Coffee is toxic. You shouldn't—"

Jessica did an about-face. "And this isn't?" She wiped a bit of chocolate off the corner of Amber's mouth and held up her finger.

"Dark chocolate works better than Prozac for depression."

"In that case, I'll order a mocha latte." Jessica held the elevator door open.

STARBUCKS WAS CROWDED. The smell of burnt coffee permeated Jessica's clothes as she waited in line. She ignored her friend's protests and ordered a caramel-mocha macchiato.

Amber just asked for a cup of hot water. She had her own tea bag.

"Grab that corner table." Jessica pointed. "I'll wait for the drinks."

Once they were settled into the dark corner, Jessica fired up her computer. "Let's review the suspects."

"Suspects?" Amber dunked a homemade tea bag up and down in her cup.

"There's you." Jessica winked. She realized she was feeling giddy from all the excitement. She shouldn't be, considering the love of her life was dead and her best friend was in intensive care. But if Lolita pulled through, Jessica promised the heavens she would never get involved with a murder again. She'd be a good girl, write her dissertation, and get a proper job.

"Me?" Amber pulled a tiny blue bottle from her purse, unscrewed the top, and pinched the dropper over her tea. "Why would I kill all those people?"

"There's that 'Teeth' guy Nick mentioned."

"What teeth guy?"

"Some mafia businessman or hitman or something." Jessica twirled a pen between her fingers. "There's that nasty intern, Sally What's-Her-Name. She did threaten me. Maybe she killed Nick because he chose me over her."

"Jealousy. The green-eyed monster." Amber sipped her tea.

"Then there's Nick's cousin—Bobby Charis. He looks exactly like Nick."

"Bobby Charis? He called the development office."

"What? Why didn't you tell me?" Jessica stared at her friend.

"I don't know . . . I didn't think of it." Amber fidgeted in her chair. "Sorry."

"What did he want?" Was she really such an airhead she didn't think Bobby Charis calling the development office was important?

"He wanted to know about Mr. Schilling's VIPER pledge."

"Oh my God. Now that Chrissy and Nick are both

dead, he must be the heir." Jessica's heart sped up. "Maybe he's the *reason* they're dead."

"You think Nick's cousin is the murderer?"

"I don't know." Jessica tapped her pen on the table. "What else did he say?"

"Nothing."

"What do you know about him?" She was desperate for more.

"Nothing." Amber bit her lip.

"Okay." Jessica tapped her computer awake. She had to get back to solving the case. "Maybe we should start with the victims. First, there was Nick's dad. He took an overdose of his heart medicine. Then there was Nick." Jessica typed their names into the document. "Detective Cormier says he was killed with the same heart medicine. So that links those two murders. Who would want to kill both Nick and his dad? Mrs. Schilling, that's who."

"But she died, too." Amber said.

"Right." Jessica sipped her coffee. "Who killed her?"

"She died in New York and not in Chicago." Amber dug in her purse until she pulled out an oversized super-dark chocolate bar. "Want some?" She broke off a square and handed it across the table. "This chocolate is infused with omega-3 fatty acids for extra brain power." She took a bite straight off the bar.

"I could use extra brainpower." Jessica thought of her dissertation and the ticking clock counting the days until she got expelled. With her front teeth, she snapped off a piece of the square. Waxy bitterness exploded onto her tongue. "Who would want Chrissy Schilling dead?" she asked as she chewed.

Amber shrugged. "The cousin?"

"And why was Chrissy posing as an old lady wanting to donate to the university?"

"What?" Amber's mouth froze in a perfect oval.

"I'm betting the 'Mrs. Vandermeer' you met was really Mrs. Schilling wearing a silver wig. Or maybe she dyed her hair. You said her face was young and pretty, right?" Jessica took a swig of macchiato to wash down the bitter chocolate.

"It was dyed for sure. But why—"

"Maybe she wanted to frame you."

"What? I don't even know her."

"Maybe she knew your tea bags were suspected in Nick's dad's murder. So maybe she wanted to make it look like you'd killed them both."

"How would she know that?" Amber scrunched up her face. "I'm not following."

"Okay. Let's say Chrissy Schilling killed her husband using an overdose of his digitalis. And then she found out the cops suspected your tea. So, she got you to come to the Parker Hotel, took more of your tea bags, and set the scene in Nick's room so it appeared he had tea with you, too."

"But my tea bags aren't poison." Amber shook her head. "It was frog juice." Her hand flew to her mouth.

"What?" Jessica narrowed her brows. "What's frog juice?"

"Batrachotoxin." Amber averted her gaze. "Detective Cormier said that's what really killed them—Mr. Schilling, Mrs. Schilling, and Lolita's grandmother."

Batrachotoxin. Where have I heard that before? Then it came to her.

"Gary!" Jessica blurted out.

"Gary wouldn't hurt anyone." Amber popped a curl into her mouth.

"Come on. Who else would have poisonous frog juice?" Jessica scrutinized her friend. "But . . . Nick was killed with digitalis, right? So how do we explain *his* death?"

Amber crinkled her nose and shrugged.

"Did Nick's dad have an overdose of digitalis *and* batrachotoxin in his bloodstream?" Jessica asked, chewing the cuticle of her index finger. "How would Chrissy Schilling get ahold of frog juice?"

"I don't know!" Amber tapped on her own head.

"Maybe the murders have something to do with those Romanov jewels. Or the money laundering?" Jessica scratched her head. "I mean, if Mr. Schilling was using the museum to sell stuff, maybe something went wrong—"

Amber bit her lip. "I think Detective Cormier mentioned Chrissy Schilling had jewels in her purse, along with my tea bags."

"So she was after the jewels." Jessica gritted her

teeth in concentration. "And the inheritance, of course. But then why is she dead? And if there was frog juice in the tea somehow—"

"There's no frog juice in my tea!"

"Just humor me for a minute." Jessica took a sip of coffee. "If Chrissy drank frog juice, she would have died in Chicago, not New York. So, the poison had to be delivered through some other means. Maybe that witch Sally What's-Her-Name poisoned Nick and the rest of his family. But why? Did she want the jewels? Or the job?"

"None of it makes sense." Amber shook her head. "Detective Cormier did say if they could figure out how the poison was administrated, they'd have a better chance at catching the killer."

"Right. We have to figure out how the frog juice was administered." Jessica tapped her fingers on the table. "How did all of these people connected with the Center end up ingesting batrachotoxin?" She narrowed her eyes. "And why would Chrissy Schilling disguise herself to ask about VIPERs?"

For a moment, Amber's mouth formed a perfect oval, and then she said, "She mostly wanted to know how to get *out* of a VIPER agreement. I think she was trying to find out how a spouse could break the pledge—"

Aha! "That's it." Jessica nodded. "She wanted to know how to break her husband's pledge to the Center and take all the money and paintings for herself. Unless the cousin killed Mr. Schilling, Chrissy, and Nick for the inheritance . . .

Amber's phone chimed, and she rummaged through her fat purse until she found it. As she listened to the voice message, the color drained from her face.

"What?" Jessica asked.

"Gary." Her eyes widened like a deer in headlights. "He's been in an accident."

"What? Where?"

"He went to West Virginia to help rescue his little brother. And now he's in critical condition." She dug in her purse again, this time pulling out a tiny vial. "His mom left a message." She unscrewed the cap and took a swig directly from the bottle. "I've got to go down there."

"I'm going with you." Jessica downed the rest of her macchiato and stood up. "Your boyfriend has got some explaining to do."

26

Ten minutes later, Jessica white-knuckled the armrest while Amber swerved around corners and zipped through yellow lights. "If you don't slow down, Gary and Lolita won't be the only ones in the hospital."

"Gary's in the hospital because he saved all those kids." Amber slammed on the brakes to avoid hitting a truck. "He's a hero."

"What was he doing in West Virginia?" Jessica double-checked her seat belt.

"His brother and some other kids were touring the mine where his dad and grandfather worked." Amber gunned through the next intersection. "They got trapped by floodwaters. Gary went down to get them out. He's an expert spelunker and knows those caves inside and out. Good thing, too. The kids were so dehydrated that they wouldn't have lasted much longer." She swerved to miss a lady crossing the street.

"Where are you going?" Jessica cranked her head around to see the freeway exit disappearing in the distance. "West Virginia is that way." She pointed over her shoulder.

"I promised Amira I'd bring her some paints." Amber yanked on the steering wheel. "It won't take long. She's such a troubled soul—I don't want to break my promise."

"Amira?" Jessica wondered how Amber could be so upset about Gary one minute and running errands the next. Sometimes her priorities were a little screwy.

"She's one of my Girls First students. You should come in and meet her. She's a talented artist." The tires squealed as Amber turned into a parking lot. "Come on." She reached around and grabbed a bag from the back seat.

Jessica followed her friend into the plain brick school building. The hallway was decorated with pictures: girls of all colors and shapes wearing saris and bright head scarfs, jeans and hijabs. In the distance, girls' voices raised in a rousing chorus of *Twinkle, Twinkle, Little Star.* Jessica was conscious of her boots clicking on the floor tiles and tried to soften her step.

Amber knocked on the second door on the left and then entered the classroom. Jessica followed. Six little girls sat on a carpet in a circle, and a teenager sat alone in a corner, drawing. All the girls were deep in concentration, coloring letters of the alphabet and animals corresponding to each: *A is for Ape, B is for Bear, C is for Cat* . . .

A young blonde woman interrupted their work. "Say hello to Miss Bush." Five of the girls followed orders, greeting Amber in unison. A teenager with long dark braids and severe eyebrows didn't look up from her art work. The teacher and Amber exchanged a meaningful look.

"Amira, how are you, sweetie?" Amber said as she sat down next to the teen. "Look how pretty you color!" She waved at Jessica. "Come and look at what Amira made."

Jessica joined Amber and knelt down next to the shy girl. She couldn't believe the teenager could draw with such precision and passion. "Wow. This is amazing." Jessica gazed down at the finely detailed bombed-out buildings and the bloodied faces of children. It dawned on her that the girl was drawing from memory, and her heart nearly broke. She plopped onto the floor, sliding her phone from her pocket. "I like art, too." She scrolled through her photos until she found a picture she'd taken of Nikolai Prisekin's *Hard Times* at the Center.

"She doesn't talk," Amber whispered into Jessica's ear. "Ever since she and her mother escaped the war in Syria."

Jessica showed Amira the Prisekin painting, a horse-drawn wagon being bombed by war planes. Amira gazed down with interest. Jessica then scrolled to Kandinsky's *Cannons*.

Amira grabbed Jessica's phone and held it close to her face, staring at the colorful abstract image—off-kilter buildings floating in a desert of yellow, brown, and blue.

"I study art," Jessica said. "Why painters paint and what their paintings mean."

The girl peered up at Jessica with serious brown eyes. "I want to be a painter."

Amber gasped.

The teacher crossed the room to join them. "What did you say, Amira?"

Amira picked up a blue colored pencil and resumed drawing.

"This is one of my favorites," Jessica said, pulling up Marianne von Werefkin's eerie *Self-Portrait*.

Amira studied the artist's huge neck, yellow cheeks, and glowing red eyes. "*Sahira-ton*," she whispered.

Jessica glanced up at the teacher, who only shrugged.

"*Sahira*," repeated a little girl sitting nearby. "It means witch."

"I brought you some watercolors." Amber reached into her bag and handed the set to Amira.

Amira smiled and held out another drawing. This one had several teenage girls and some older men on what looked like an airplane. The girls were in different stages of undress.

"What is this?" Jessica asked. She grimaced and glanced over at Amber.

Amber grabbed the picture out of the girl's hands. "Did some men take you on an airplane?"

Amira lowered her gaze but refused to speak.

"Gary was right!" Amber dropped the sketch pad onto the floor. "We've got to tell Detective Cormier. I didn't believe him. I thought Mr. Schilling was helping—"

"This isn't what I think it is, is it?" Jessica whispered, caressing the top of Amira's head. "Can I look at your art, honey?"

Amira handed her the pad. Jessica flipped through scene after scene of bombings and bloody, fragmented people, and young girls with older men. They made her skin crawl. She stopped cold when she got to a picture of a gray-haired man wearing a suit—a knife stabbed through his heart. The girl holding the knife looked a lot like Amira. *Holy shit!* Jessica glanced over at the girl. *Could she have killed Mr. Schilling and the other donors?* Her heart sped up at the thought. The poor sweet girl was only a teenager.

"Look at this," Jessica whispered to Amber.

"I can't believe I didn't see it before." Amber's lip was trembling. "I made a terrible mistake."

"One reason bad people get away with things like this is because kids aren't believed, even by good, well-intentioned people." Jessica put a hand on her friend's shoulder. "It's not your fault," she said, even though she couldn't believe her friend had been so gullible. *What in the hell did she think the old pervert was doing with teenage girls for God's sake?* It made her stomach sour.

"Let's go." Amber grabbed her shopping bag and distributed new Crayolas and chocolate bars to the rest of the girls. She turned to the teacher. "I have to go out of town on a family emergency, but I should be back in time for my class next week."

After receiving hugs, Amber gathered up her monster purse and headed out of the classroom. "See you next week!"

Jessica was about to take off after her when the teacher touched her arm. "You should consider volunteering. You could teach them art."

"I'm a philosopher, not an artist."

"Whatever you are, you're a natural teacher. You're the only person who has gotten Amira to speak."

Jessica smiled. "Maybe I will." She did love teaching, and teaching refugee girls was far more appealing than teaching sorority girls. She studied Amira's artwork. The girl holding the knife in the drawing looked a lot like Amira. "Some men are exploiting those girls."

Amber's eyes widened. "I'm so stupid—I should have realized what was going on. That's why some of the girls would disappear for days." Amber crinkled her nose. "Not some men. Richard Schilling."

"You think he flew them to New York on his private jet for his rich friends?" Jessica felt sick at the thought.

Amber's hand trembled as she reached inside her

purse. "I don't know. Right now, we have to make it to West Virginia. At least since Mr. Schilling's dead, we don't have to worry about that happening anymore."

"But what if he was working with others? Maybe he was blackmailing one of them. That would be a motive for murder. I'm going to call Detective Cormier." Jessica pulled her phone out of her pocket, along with the detective's card. She tapped in the number, but it went directly to voice mail.

AFTER FIVE HOURS on Interstate 90, Jessica's butt was tired. She needed to get out and stretch her legs. She pointed at a sign for Cuyahoga Valley National Park. "Can we stop for a few minutes?"

The only snacks they had were chocolate bars and herbal tinctures from Amber's ample purse. Jessica craved a nice big stack of banana nut pancakes with whipped cream.

For the last hour, Amber had been encouraging her to ditch her current dissertation and write about art therapy instead.

"I really think you should," Amber said as she parked the car.

"I don't know." Jessica inhaled the scent of trees. "I'd have to start my research all over again. And I barely have two months." The sound of rushing water drew her toward a trailhead. The smell of cedars cleared her head. She inhaled deeply.

Then a firecracker went off in her brain. "Maybe I could end my dissertation on art therapy!" *That's it! That's the answer.* She'd been having such trouble writing the last chapter. The whole dissertation had seemed pointless, so disconnected from anything real. But if she could connect her discussion of Nietzsche and Russian art to the refugee girls and art therapy . . . Suddenly, she was looking forward to getting back to writing. *Maybe Nietzsche was right: Without art, we'd die of life.*

"We have another three hours until Morgantown, so we can't stop for long." Amber followed close on Jessica's heels. "On top of everything else, I have a paper due in English lit, and the stupid professor insists on a hard copy. Can you drive the rest of the way while I proofread? I'll have to mail it from West Virginia."

"Sure," Jessica said as she read the trail markers. "There's a waterfall in less than a quarter of a mile. Let's go see it. It will only take a few minutes, and I really need a break."

Stepping over roots and rocks, Jessica wished she'd worn her hiking boots instead of her cowboy boots. "I *could* write on art therapy." Saying it out loud gave her another idea. Maybe she could work for the Center, running educational programs especially for refugees. "I wonder if Mr. Schilling's donation to the Center is valid."

"Why wouldn't it be?" Amber lifted her flowing paisley skirt as she stepped over a fallen branch. "He signed it."

"And he stipulated that part of it go to refugees, right?" Jessica stopped and turned back to face her friend. "No one knows you put that there . . ."

Amber nodded and popped the end of a snaky lock of hair into her mouth. "I think it depends on whether his heir or heirs go along with the pledge and don't revoke it. Unless it was in his will." She bit her lip.

The air was cooler next to the waterfall. Jessica stood in silence, admiring the oxidized rocks and the foamy water rushing over them. She closed her eyes and listened to the power of the water crashing into the pool from twenty feet above. She missed Montana and the mountains . . . and her mom. To pull herself from the brink of melancholy, she willed herself to melt into the moment and become one with the smell of damp rocks and the chorus of forest birds.

She opened her eyes, taking in the vibrant green leaves and grasses and the rust-colored rocks. She would write her dissertation and get her degree if it was the last thing she did. She was determined. When she got back to Chicago, she'd stay up night and day until she finished.

"We'd better get going." Amber's voice brought her back from her meditations.

Jessica nodded and took one long last sip of cool,

clean air. With renewed confidence and commitment, she strode down the path and back to the car.

By the time they reached Pittsburgh, the flat plains had turned into rolling hills and, thanks to Amber and the refugee girls, Jessica felt alive.

THREE HOURS LATER, Jessica pulled into the parking garage for Morgantown General Hospital. It was almost midnight, pitch dark, and Amber was doubtful visiting hours were open. The ICU was on the third floor. As they rode the elevator up, Amber tapped on her head. She took slow, deep breaths. *In through the nose . . . out through the mouth.*

When she'd called for an update two hours ago, she'd been told Gary was barely hanging on, and she was scared. *What if he dies?* She shivered. After rescuing the last of the boys, Gary had been crushed by a cave-in. He was a hero. She should be proud of him. Instead, she wished he'd never gone in the first place.

As she exited the elevator, Amber dug out her Rescue Remedy and took the maximum dose. The lighting was dim, and the quiet of the hallway was punctuated with beeping sounds coming from the hospital rooms. Just that morning, she'd been in another ICU, visiting Lolita. She prayed to the Goddess that both Lolita and Gary would pull through. Then she and Gary could take a mini-vacation. They could go away for a weekend and get a cabin on Lake Michigan and do nothing but cuddle.

Jessica pointed to a sign for ICU, and they entered a waiting room. A family of five slept in recliners and a couch in one corner of the room. There was an alcove with a mini refrigerator and coffee at one end near an intercom with a big sign that read "Buzz for entry."

While Jessica rummaged around in a mini fridge, Amber pressed the intercom button and asked if she could visit Gary. The nurse buzzed her in, saying, "No more than ten minutes, and no more than two visitors at one time."

Each room resembled a circuit board. Wires and cables ran from patient to various machines, registering vital information on computer screens manned by nurses. Closed curtains shielded some rooms from view, while others were exposed. A nurse led Amber to a small glassed-in room with a curtain around the bed.

Gary lay in bed, hooked up to fluid bags hanging like overripe fruit from IV trees on either side. He was wearing an oxygen mask, and his wan skin matched the pale white walls. Amber felt terrible he was all alone. His mother had been there earlier but had to go home to take care of Gary's little brother, who'd suffered minor injuries in the cave-in.

Amber fought back tears as she approached the side of the bed. When she touched the back of his hand, his eyes flickered open. She smiled, but tears fell onto the bedsheet.

"You came," he said weakly. The mask muffled his voice.

She nodded. "Of course."

"I'm sorry." He dragged his hand up to the mask and moved it to one side.

"It's not your fault." She stroked his hair.

Gary tried to lift his head, but it fell back on the pillow. "I have to tell you something. Now. Before..." His voice was hoarse.

"Jessica's here, too."

Amber glanced at her friend, who was standing at the back of the small room.

"I did—" Gary said, gasping for breath.

"Shhh . . ." Amber put her fingers to her lips. "You're tired. Don't try to talk. You're going to be fine." She looked around to see if the nurse was within earshot. *I should have come alone.* She didn't know what Gary might confess to, but she didn't want anyone else to hear. Especially not her sleuthing friend.

"GARY?" Jessica moved closer to the bed. "What did you do?"

He closed his eyes. "I only meant Schilling, not the others . . ." His voice trailed off.

"Nick," Jessica whispered. *Wait.* Nick had been killed with digitalis, not frog juice. "Did you kill Nick?"

"No." Gary's eyes flashed open. "Not Nick." His face

reddened and his forehead shone with sweat. "Richard Schilling. He deserved to die, the heartless bastard." Spit formed at the corners of his mouth, like a rabid dog.

"Mr. Schilling?" Jessica paced the length of the room. "But how? In Amber's tea bags?" If she had put the pieces together correctly, then both batrachotoxin *and* digitalis had been present in Mr. Schilling's bloodstream. Nick's had only digitalis. And Chrissy and the Countess had only batrachotoxin.

Gary struggled for breath.

"Don't talk," Amber said, caressing his hand. "You need to rest." Her eyes were wet with tears.

Jessica stopped pacing and turned back to Gary. "You poisoned him with batrachotoxin from your frogs. But how?"

Gary whispered something, and Amber moved the oxygen mask back over his nose and mouth.

"Who killed Nick?" Jessica moved to the bedside and stared down at the helpless man. "If you didn't do it . . . ?" There had to be two killers. Gary and someone else, someone who'd used the digitalis. Chrissy Schilling? Sally What's-Her-Name? Amira?

Gary closed his eyes again.

The nurse appeared at the curtain. "Time to go, ladies."

"How long has she been there?" Amber whispered as they left the room. "Do you think she heard?"

"I doubt it matters." By the looks of it, Gary didn't

have long. He'd just confessed to murder, so maybe it was better this way. It didn't feel better. Even though he was a killer, Jessica felt sorry for him . . . and for poor Amber.

Amber's eyes sprouted tears. Jessica put an arm around her and led the way back to the waiting room. She deposited Amber in a reclining chair, then went to search for some tissues. There was a box next to the small refrigerator. She opened the fridge, peeked inside, grabbed a couple string cheeses and two bottles of water, and carried the haul back to the recliners. She handed the box of tissues and a water bottle to Amber.

The silence made the waiting room feel like a mausoleum. The air smelled of sour milk. Jessica buttoned her fringe jacket against the air-conditioning and munched on a string cheese. Its chewy, salty, smoothness was comforting. She held out the other cheese to Amber, who shook her head and blew her nose.

Jessica needed to get back in to see Gary before he died. He wouldn't last long. His lungs had collapsed, and his condition was touch-and-go. *How did he administer the frog juice? And why did he kill Chrissy and the Countess?* She needed to find out what had happened while she could.

Amber dug in her mammoth purse and pulled out a purple vial. She filled the pipette with brown liquid and dropped it into one bottle, then the other. "This will help," she sniffled.

Jessica took a sip and closed her eyes. Despite knowing Gary's time was short, she found herself fighting to stay awake. Exhausted, she fell into a fitful sleep.

JESSICA BLINKED HER EYES OPEN. *How long was I out?* Only half awake, she glanced over to check on Amber. Her friend was gone. *Or am I dreaming?* She tried to force herself to wake up but couldn't. Her eyelids weighed a ton. She couldn't keep them open. Resistance was futile. *The purple vial. The brown liquid.* She drifted back to sleep.

27

Amber waited until Jessica was asleep before tiptoeing back into the ICU. She pushed the button and waited for a nurse to buzz her in.

As she opened the door, the nurse asked, "Are you Amber?"

Amber nodded.

"He's been asking for you." The nurse led her back to Gary's alcove.

Except for the light flashing on the pain med machine and the screen monitoring his vitals above his head, the room was dark. Gary was pale and still. She silently crossed the room and sat her purse in the chair. She stroked his forehead. He was warm. Alive. *Thank the Goddess.*

"Gary, honey, I'm here." She scooted the chair closer to the bed, moved her purse, and sat down.

"Amber," he whispered. "I'm sorry."

She forced a smile. She had to be strong for his sake. "You'll be okay. You'll see." She rummaged in her purse and pulled out her Rescue Remedy and another vial, small and brown. She administered a few drops of RR under her own tongue, then set the blue vial on the bed table. "Open your mouth."

Like a baby bird, he opened. She counted out ten drops.

"What is it? Tastes like brandy."

"That's because it is brandy, laced with arnica for healing."

"You're so sweet." He reached for her hand.

"When you recover, we should go to the ocean together." She lifted his hand to her lips. It was so cold it made her shiver.

"I'd like that." He gave her a weak smile. "Seeing you is the best medicine."

She wanted to ask him about the poison, but she didn't know how to bring it up. She glanced around to make sure the nurse wasn't nearby. "You shouldn't have told Jessica."

"I had to." He squeezed her hand. "I don't want you taking the blame."

"But you'll go to jail." She couldn't help it. Tears flowed down her cheeks. She wiped at them with the sleeve of her sweater.

"I've ruined everything, haven't I?" He had a sad, faraway look in his eyes.

"Don't say that." She leaned in and kissed his cheek.

He smelled vinegary, like he was fermenting. She tapped the air just above his head to balance his energy. She was determined to heal him even if it meant he went to prison for life. Given his mental state, maybe he would get a lighter sentence. *Maybe he'll get out early on good behavior. I can wait for him.*

"Richard Schilling was messing with your refugee girls. Something snapped." Gary sighed. "First Julie . . ." His voice trailed off.

"You were right. I should have listened." She nodded and continued tapping. "He was a creep."

"Schilling mines killed my grandfather and my father." He pushed the control for the electric bed and sat up. "And then that bastard took Julie."

"I know." Even though her arm was getting tired, she continued her energy work, encouraged he was sitting up. In the past, whenever she'd asked about his sister, Julie, he always got so upset.

"When I heard the bastard was taking advantage of those girls, I had to stop him." He gazed at her with sad eyes.

"Yeah." She dropped her tired hands into her lap. "I have a confession." Amber wrapped a lock of hair around her index finger. "I added a clause to his VIPER agreement with the Center."

"What?" Gary smiled.

"For the refugees. I put it in his pledge." She rubbed her hands together.

"Clever girl." Gary held out his hand and she took it.

She bounced up and down in the chair. "He signed it."

"Maybe his money can go some distance in repairing the damage he's done." Gary caressed her hand.

She lifted his hand to her lips and kissed it—tubes, tape, and all. "It's not fair." She started crying. "I don't want to lose you."

"Don't cry." He took her hand in both of his. "I'm tougher than I look."

She giggled through her tears.

He fell back against the pillow and closed his eyes. "Maybe I should sleep now."

She nodded, sniffling. "I'll be back in the morning."

"You get some rest, too." He gazed at her again, tears pooling in his eyes. "I love you, sweetie."

"I love you, too." When she bent down and kissed his lips, a tremor ran up her spine. He was so cold. She rummaged in her purse and pulled out a small zip-lock full of tea bags. "These are warming. Have the nurse make you a cup."

Still holding her gaze, he nodded. A tear rolled down his cheek.

She dabbed his cheek with a tissue, then kissed the same spot. "Rest now, lovey." She smiled at him. "I'll be back with Twisted Twix."

As she left his room, she thought of their first night together, mashing Twix bars, pretzels, and chocolate syrup into a treat all their own. She'd beat him at chess, and that's when he'd asked her to stay the night.

She tiptoed back into the waiting room. Jessica was sound asleep, curled up in one of the recliners. Amber slid into the recliner next to her. She reached into her purse for some calming lozenges and a square of chocolate. She'd run out of RR.

She closed her eyes and said a silent prayer to the universe. *What will I do if he doesn't make it? What will happen if he does?* He would go to prison or worse. She shuddered. *Richard Schilling was a horrible man, but did Gary need to kill him? And what about the others?* Whatever he'd done, she couldn't help loving him.

The lozenge wasn't working. Her heart was racing. *Panic attack.* She tapped the air, remotely realigning Gary's chi. She envisioned him surrounded by healing energy. She tried to focus all of her anxiety into willing him better.

After another hour twisting and turning, trying to get comfortable and calm down, Amber unzipped the secret compartment in her purse and removed the prescription bottle. She hated to resort to pharmaceuticals, but she was desperate. She glanced over at Jessica, twisted the top, and tapped out a little purple football, then another for good measure. She popped them into her mouth and held them under her tongue. The familiar sweetness calmed her, and she imagined the powerful drug coursing through her blood like rays of sunshine through the leaves of a magnolia tree.

SOMEONE WAS SHAKING HER SHOULDER.

"I'm awake! I'm awake!" Amber sat up in the chair. "What's happening?" When she opened her eyes, she felt a wave of nausea. She needed more sleep.

"Amber?"

Her vision came into focus and she recognized the nurse speaking to her.

"Gary," Amber whispered. Her hand flew to her mouth, and terror pierced her heart.

"I'm so sorry." The nurse squatted down so she was at eye level. "His heart stopped. We couldn't revive him."

"No," Amber whimpered. "No, no, no . . ." She broke down sobbing.

JESSICA PUSHED cold scrambled eggs around on her plate. The hospital cafeteria was in the basement and felt like a tomb. The fluorescent lights were too bright. They made her head hurt, and she had a painful crick in her neck from sleeping in that chair.

Amber looked even worse than Jessica felt. Her eyes had been swollen and red from crying ever since the nurse gave them the news.

"I loved him . . ." Amber whimpered, putting her

head in her hands. Her auburn curls fell down around her arms like a shroud.

"I'm so sorry." Jessica scooted her chair next to her friend and slung an arm around her. She knew what it was like to lose someone you loved. *Dad, Mike, Nick . . .* She sighed. So much grief. So much loss. Once more, she thought of Nietzsche. *"To live is to suffer. To survive is to find meaning in the suffering."*

How do people go on? She thought of Amira, drawing pictures of her bombed-out house and dead neighbors. Maybe Nietzsche was right. *Maybe art makes the suffering bearable.*

"It's Mr. Schilling's fault!" Amber lifted her tearstained face and pounded on the table. "The mines. The girls."

Poor Amber. Jessica watched her melt into another puddle of tears. "What do you mean?"

Amber just shook her head and bawled.

Jessica offered her a piece of chocolate. "Come on, Amber, you've got to eat something."

Amber shook her head again.

"Do you want to visit his family before we head back to Chicago?"

She nodded.

"Why don't you go get cleaned up." Jessica wanted to get rid of Amber long enough to call Detective Cormier and pass along Gary's confession. She still needed to figure out how he'd done it.

Almost as if she'd heard Jessica's thoughts, Amber

said, "We can't tell anyone about what Gary did. It would kill his mom. She's suffered enough." She sniffled into a sodden tissue.

"But the murder investigation . . . I should tell Detective Cormier."

"No!" Amber was trembling. "Please don't." Her shoulders were shaking again, and she broke down sobbing. "Please," she pleaded. She had a look of sheer panic in her eyes.

"Okay, okay." Jessica put her arms around her soggy friend. "I won't tell anyone."

"Promise me!" Amber raised her face and stared into Jessica's eyes. "Promise you won't tell anyone."

Jessica bit her lip. How could she promise? She had to tell the detective about Gary. *Even if Richard and Chrissy were bad people, did they deserve to be poisoned? And the Countess, Lolita's grandmother—she was wonderful.* Even if that had been an accident . . . what a waste. She stared into her desperate friend's bloodshot eyes and took a breath.

"I promise." She shook her head. There were no good choices here. Right now, she had to take care of her friend.

"Thank you." Amber slumped back into the chair.

Gary's childhood home was a clapboard cottage in the suburbs of Morgantown. His mother came to the door wearing a baby blue floral muumuu. The curve of her wide back spoke volumes about the burdens she'd carried in her life. Her face lit up when she saw Amber.

"Mercy me." She held her hands together in supplication. "Thank God, you came. I was just getting ready to go to the hospital."

A lump formed in Jessica's throat. *Hasn't anyone called her yet?*

When Amber broke into tears, Gary's mother's eyes widened. Her face went as white as the milkweed growing around the front stoop. "What is it, girl? What happened?"

Amber shook her head and wrapped her arms around the stunned woman.

Jessica felt like a third wheel. She took a step backwards and nearly fell off the porch. Watching the two women cling to each other brought tears to her eyes.

After a few more minutes of shock and sobs, Gary's mother—Viola—invited them in for coffee. Even Amber took a chipped ceramic mug and sipped black coffee as they sat around a small Formica table in the back corner of the kitchen.

The three women stared at each other in silence. The bitterness of the strong coffee seemed appropriate. Jessica glanced around the room. The stained linoleum and dented refrigerator had seen better days. So had Gary's mom. To avoid the smell of bacon fat and sour mop water, Jessica held her coffee cup under her nose.

Viola disappeared into the bathroom. She sounded

like a goose honking. She reappeared, carrying a box of tissues, and fell back into her chair. "Gary was a good boy."

Amber nodded. "He was special."

"He was a good boy," Viola repeated, wiping her eyes with a tissue. "I know God has his reasons, but now I ain't got no one left." She broke down.

Amber moved her chair closer and put her arm around Viola. Heads touching, they both bawled.

Jessica stared into her coffee cup, trying not to cry.

"Richard Schilling is dead," Amber said, finally. She wiped her nose on her sweater sleeve.

"Richard Schilling . . ." Viola's mouth hung open. She obviously knew him.

Jessica's mind was racing a mile a minute. How could Viola Calloway know Nick's dad?

"He owns the mine," Viola said. She got up and leaned on the stove, turning her back to them. "I worked in the office." She held on to the edges of the stove like her life depended on it. "I've never told anyone this before, but he would visit the mine every year . . . and when he did, he'd make me go out with him. He threatened to fire me. And Frank, too." Like a zombie, she slowly walked over to the coffee maker, picked up the pot, and topped off their cups.

"When I got pregnant, everyone thought the baby was Frank's." She put the pot back on the coffee maker and shuffled back to her chair. "But Gary didn't look anything like Frank."

Whoa. Jessica picked at her jacket. How could anyone be sure who their father was? *How can anyone be sure of anything?* Even motherhood wasn't certain anymore. She thought of last year and that wacko genetic scientist implanting college coeds' eggs in rich women's bodies. She cringed. She still couldn't believe she'd been one of those college coeds.

Still, biology wasn't destiny. And blood wasn't love.

Viola took a sip from her cup. "I could have put up with it to save my job, but when that dirty bastard took Julie . . ." Her voice trailed off. "She was only sixteen, for God's sake." Her shoulders shook with silent sobs. "Julie insisted she wanted to go. And the cops did nothing to find her. They thought I was hysterical and she'd just run away. Of course they'd think that. *Mr. Schilling* was filthy rich . . . the biggest employer in town. The cops wouldn't go after him. They didn't care . . ."

Jessica felt sick. *What had Nick's father done to this woman? To this family?* Her hand was trembling as she picked up her cup.

Viola pointed to a dime-sized pucker of skin on her arm. "He smoked cigars."

Jessica shuddered. Trying to control her own rage, she asked, "Who's Julie?"

"Julie is my only daughter. Gary's younger sister." Viola's gaze was searing. "Richard took her four years ago, and I haven't seen her since."

The trip home was somber. Jessica drove eight hours straight while Amber slept in the back seat.

Should I call Detective Cormier? Would it break my promise to give him a hint? She thought of Kant's classic example of lying to protect someone from being killed. *Do I betray my friend and solve the murder, or do I keep my promise and hide the truth?*

With Gary dead, it wasn't a question of bringing a killer to justice or locking him up to prevent other murders. But keeping quiet would leave Lolita without answers—without closure—about her grandmother. *Is that okay?*

On the other hand, the world was rid of a horrible man who'd exploited the vulnerable. That was a good thing. *Isn't that justice?*

"Can we drop off my English paper on campus?" Amber was awake. She rubbed her eyes, then fished a big white envelope out of her purse.

Jessica glanced over at her friend. "Sure."

Amber stuffed her paper into the envelope. She was about to lick the seal—

"Wait!" Jessica screamed. "Don't lick that!" She nearly hit the car next to her. She slammed on the brakes and skidded onto the shoulder of the highway, gravel flying and tires screeching. Jessica's heart galloped. "Let me see that envelope." She held out her hand.

Amber gave her a quizzical look. "What's wrong?"

"Give it to me!"

"Okay, okay. Calm down." Amber held it out.

"That's how he did it." Jessica snatched the envelope and sniffed the seal. The acrid odor assaulted her nose. "He put the frog juice on the envelopes. When the donors licked them, they got poisoned."

"What?" Amber stared at her, mouth hanging open.

"Gary killed the VIPER donors using these envelopes. That's how he administered the poison." Jessica shook her head. "That's how he did it."

"No." Amber was trembling. "I could have . . . I was just trying to get rid of the old envelopes from the office so they wouldn't go to waste."

Jessica nodded. "You would have died." Holding the envelope by the corner, she carefully set it on the console between the two seats. "I've got to deliver this to Detective Cormier."

"But you promised!"

"I'm sorry, but this is evidence."

"What about my English paper?" Amber sucked on her hair.

Jessica scowled as she gingerly lifted the envelope and shook her friend's homework out onto the floor. "We've got to take this to Detective Cormier. Now."

"I can't." Amber's eyes welled up. "Please. Can you drop me off?" Tears rolled down her cheeks. "I can't betray Gary. I loved him."

"I'll take your car and bring it back later."

Amber nodded. She wiped her eyes on her sleeve.

"I'll turn in your English paper on my way back."

Jessica gave her friend a weak smile. "You should get some rest."

Jessica knew the questions buzzing in her brain wouldn't let her rest for a long time. She looked over her shoulder and pulled back onto the highway.

28

Finally, summer had given way to fall. The cool breeze off the lake revived Jessica—she hoped the long walk to Blind Faith would help clear her head. She detoured to Lake Michigan. The white-caps churned as far as her eye could see. They reflected the churning thoughts inside her mind.

She had just over one month to finish her dissertation. She stared out across the expanse of gray water and listened to the waves slapping the rocky shore. She'd done so much research. But none of it seemed important anymore. She wanted her dissertation to make a difference. She wanted philosophy to matter. She thought of Amira and the other refugee girls. With new resolve, she picked up her pace and headed inland.

By the time Jessica reached Blind Faith, she was sticky with sweat. She threw her backpack into her usual booth and slid in after it. Strong coffee and banana nut pancakes. That's what she needed. She waved to the dog-collared waitress, then pulled her computer from her pack and tapped it awake.

After two double lattes and a stack of pancakes—extra whipped cream—she'd written ten more pages on the value of art as therapy.

If life is suffering, then we need do more than just survive. We need to thrive. And to thrive, we need to make suffering meaningful through art, whatever that may be, including writing a dissertation in philosophy.

The words raced out of her fingers. She couldn't type fast enough.

FOR THE NEXT MONTH, Jessica devoured almost as many pancakes as she did books on art therapy. When she wasn't eating, reading, or teaching, she was writing. At first, the words came in fits and starts, as choppy as whitecaps, but later they flowed as smooth as glass.

The world slipped away . . . and she forgot about frog juice, and murder, and Nick. Instead, her thoughts flooded out, page after page, filling the blankness with something she never knew she had inside her—the power to create another world, not as it was, but as it could be.

A month later, Jessica had turned in her dissertation, applied for a position at the Center for Russian Art and Culture, and signed up to volunteer at Girls First. Finally, she collapsed into a heap on her futon. She slept for twenty-eight hours.

Then, groggy from a full day in bed, she rubbed her eyes and picked up her phone from her nightstand. *Crapulence!* She was meeting Lolita and Amber for dinner at Pavlov's in half an hour. She jumped out of bed, then made the mistake of sniffing her armpit. There was no time for a shower, so she took a quick sponge bath, then threw on one of her great-grandmother's vintage dresses—deep blue gaberdine with delicate black velvet flowers. She wriggled into her black tights and stuffed her feet into her red cowboy boots.

I hope bedhead's still in style. Her messy nest of hair was hopeless. She grabbed her wallet, phone, and keys, then headed out the door.

Her friends were waiting for her. It was a Friday night, and the restaurant was bustling. She made her way past the lineup of adventurous college students and old Russian couples waiting for tables.

"Sorry I'm late." She slid into a barstool next to Lolita. "I overslept."

"What did you do to your hair?" Lolita asked. "It looks like something the cat dragged in."

"I like it!" Amber gushed. "You look like a movie star coming home after a night out."

"And on her way to rehab," Lolita added. "Speaking

of . . . what are we drinking?" She waved at Vanya, who was chatting up a redhead at the end of the bar.

Vanya bounded over like a nervous cat, grabbing three shot glasses on his way. "On the roof," he said as he poured three shots of vodka.

Jessica smiled at her two best friends. Amber was healing from her grief. Lolita had recovered from the gunshot wound.

"I'm guessing he means on the house, in which case, set up another row." Lolita tapped on the bar with a red fingernail. "Carrot Top's a bit young for you, isn't she, Cousin Vanya?"

"Is business, not pleasure." He chuckled.

"Why do we get free drinks?" Amber asked.

"Because Lolita survived and Sergei is in prison."

"I'll drink to that!" Lolita raised her glass. "What doesn't kill me makes me stronger."

"Nietzsche!" Jessica laughed.

"See? I know some philosophy, too." Lolita leaned sideways and bumped Jessica with her shoulder.

Jessica downed her shot, then picked up the second one and held it high. "Everything decisive in life arrives amidst the greatest obstacles. I've been struggling to write my dissertation for years. Getting the degree was a reason to write, but I needed a purpose. Thanks to Amber, I found it at Girls First. To Amber." She clinked glasses with her friends and took the shot.

"Vanya, another round for another toast." Amber rotated back and forth on her barstool.

Vanya grinned and poured out three more vodkas.

"To Doctor Jessica." Amber lifted her glass.

"Whoa. Not quite yet," Jessica said. "I turned in my dissertation, but I still have to defend it."

Lolita grinned. "They'd better collect your weapons at the door."

"Let's hope my wit is sharp enough."

"It's sharper than most." A familiar whiskey tenor drifted from behind her, and she swiveled around to see Jack. His crooked smile hit her like a lightning bolt. "Hello, cowgirl." His soulful eyes held a question.

"Jack!" She'd forgotten he was being released today. She tripped over her own feet as she moved in for a hug and landed in his arms.

"I've missed you," he whispered into her hair.

She inhaled the spicy scent of smoke and soap. After two years in prison, he felt like a stranger. He'd changed. But, so had she. "I'm glad you're out."

He held her at arm's length and stared into her face. "You did it. You finished your dissertation."

She nodded. "Thanks to my friends."

"I knew you would." He took her hand. "I'm proud of you, cowgirl."

Jessica blushed. She waved to Vanya for another glass. Once all of their glasses were full, Jessica raised hers. "To friendship, the true meaning of life."

She had just downed her shot when her phone buzzed. She glanced down. *What the . . . a voicemail from Dmitry?* He'd never called her before. She tapped her phone and listened to the message. *Oh. My. God.* She tingled with excitement down to her fingertips.

"Hey, you guys!" She waved at Vanya to refill their glasses. "I got the job! I'm going to be the education director for the Center."

29

It had taken every moment of the last month, and all Dmitry's effort, but he'd managed to get the Center ready for its grand opening. The police had finally given the green light. He only hoped their investigation wouldn't cast a lasting shadow over the party.

It was no secret that one murder had put his mind at ease. His brother Sergei had been killed in jail, shanked in the yard by a rival. Hopefully, the mob would go after the killer and his gang and leave Dmitry's family alone. As far as he knew, only the crooked cop knew about Lolita's undercover work. And Detective Cormier was confident the department had enough on him to keep him locked away with his mouth shut. Dmitry hoped the detective was right. *Not many people cross Bratva and survived.* He laughed to himself. He was one of the lucky ones.

He paced the foyer again, checking on the catering and cash bar. The dainty *zakuski*—caviar on toast, pickled mushrooms and beets, and charcuterie—were pretty but didn't look very filling. Still, he trusted Sabina's judgement when it came to food, and she'd arranged for Pavlov's Banquet to cater the event. He nodded at Vanya, who was manning the bar.

Vanya gave a thumbs-up. "Showtime, boss." When he grinned, his gold grill glimmered under the track lighting. At least those tux sleeves covered up his tattoos.

Dmitry made another trip through the galleries. The Kandinskys were all framed, hanging on the wall once more. It had been a nightmare to refit the frames. Luckily, Sally Marshall, the daughter of one of their trustees, was an expert. She'd done an excellent job. And, by hiring the intern permanently, he'd secured an extra half-million dollar donation. He'd learned a few things from Bratva. As his mother used to say, "*Guba ne dura*"—lips are not stupid. In other words, know which side your bread is buttered on.

As he rounded the corner into the next gallery, he almost bumped into his daughter's friend, Jessica. She'd been hired to run the education and outreach programs.

"Ready?" she asked.

"I hope so."

"I wish Nick were here." She grimaced.

"Mr. Nick would be very proud."

She nodded. Her stiletto heels clicked on the tile floor as she ambled from one gallery to the next.

"Lolita has shoes exactly like those." He pointed to her high heels.

"These are Lolita's."

At least she isn't wearing those crazy red boots. "Have there been any more leads in the investigation?" He regretted the question as soon as he asked it. The poor girl had suffered enough. Why remind her?

"I have my hypothesis." She narrowed her eyes.

"Go on." He had his, too. *Bratva.*

"Chrissy Schilling killed Nick and his dad to get the inheritance. She used digitalis." Jessica pushed her bangs out of her face. "Richard was *also* poisoned by Gary."

"But Mrs. Schilling died, too." He put his hand to his chest. "And what about my mother?"

"Gary accidently killed them both."

"Gary?"

"Amber's boyfriend. He used batrachotoxin—frog juice." She rubbed her temples.

"*Frog* juice?" Did he hear that right? *There must be a translation problem.*

"A rare poison. Detective Cormier says they found it in the bloodstreams of three victims: Nick's dad, Chrissy, and Countess Volkova." She turned around to face him. "But he couldn't figure out how the poison was administered. It wasn't on the teacups or anywhere else in the hotel suites."

He nodded, trying to follow what she was saying.

"Well, Gary was putting it on the envelopes. So when the donors licked them to return the documents, they got poisoned. Amber almost licked one."

Dmitry mopped his brow with a handkerchief. He'd never liked licking envelopes. "Why would he want to kill donors?" He shook his head. "What did he have to gain from—"

"He only meant to kill Richard Schilling. Nick's dad owned the mine where his grandfather and father died. And, apparently, Mr. Schilling was trafficking girls . . . including Gary's sister, Julie." Arms akimbo, she stared at Dmitry with a look that could curl the hairs of a Siberian tiger. "He was a disgusting creep."

"Then how did the others die—" He took a step back.

"Gary put frog juice on the envelopes." She started pacing. "Richard got a double whammy with digitalis and frog juice. Chrissy killed him to get the inheritance. But she licked a poisoned envelope, too."

"So, my mother's death was an accident with a poisoned envelope?" Dmitry tugged at his shirt collar. The tuxedo was constricting, and he couldn't wait to get this reception over with, go home, and change into his pajamas.

"I'm sorry." Jessica bit her fingernail. "It's horrible. I think Gary had gone off the deep end."

"What a waste." He sighed. He had to stop thinking about his mother, or he'd never get through the night.

He glanced at his watch. "Doors open in five minutes. We should go."

Jessica had to take baby steps for fear of falling over in Lolita's five-inch heels. Her feet hurt, and her stomach was aflutter. She surveyed the Russian appetizers laid out on the foyer banquet table. She was too nervous to eat, even if they'd been more appealing.

She'd worn her only little black dress and put on makeup for the occasion. She still couldn't believe she had a real job. And thanks to Mr. Schilling's generous provision for refugees, and Bobby Charis' endorsement of it, she could start her special art programs. She'd already recruited Amira.

She was about to resort to a pickled beet when someone grabbed her elbow.

"Detective Cormier, what are you doing here?" Her question sounded more accusatory than she meant it to. "You came for the opening. I'm so glad."

"Actually, something's been bothering me." He led her to a quiet corner of the gallery. "I have a confession."

She got a lump in her throat. What kind of confession could a Chicago cop have for her?

"I shouldn't be telling you this." The detective paused, like maybe he'd changed his mind and wasn't going to confess after all.

"What?" Now she was dying to know.

"You didn't hear it from me, but Nick Schilling isn't dead. He's in the witness protection program."

Her mouth fell open. Her knees went weak. She thought she might pass out. She grabbed the detective's arm. "What?"

"He's going to testify against Victor "Teeth" Marsiano." He took her by the shoulders. "You've got to promise me you won't say anything. If you do, you'll put Nick's life in danger. Do you understand?"

She nodded. She was stunned. Nick was alive? Where? Could she see him? Her heart ached and felt like it might explode at the same time.

The clicking of heels on the wooden floor signaled they had company.

"Jessica, darling," Lolita purred. "What are you two doing over here in the corner, telling secrets?"

"Miss Durchenko." The detective tipped an imaginary hat. "Ladies, enjoy your evening." Detective Cormier slipped into the crowd and disappeared.

"What was that all about?" Lolita asked.

"Nothing." Jessica stumbled over the word. "He was just congratulating me."

"Yes. Congratulations, my friend." She air-kissed both cheeks. Lolita was still wearing the Bratva ring, along with a slinky silver dress and her classic red nail polish.

"Look at all the people." Jessica scanned the room, happy that folks had turned up. And now she had more reason to celebrate. In some hideout somewhere, Nick was alive. She couldn't believe it.

From across the room, a bright paisley dress caught her eye. *Amber!* To avoid slipping on the polished floor, Jessica tottered on her toes towards the purple bull's-eye.

Jack stood next to the hippy hacker, looking sexy in a nerdy sort of way in his wrinkled navy-blue jacket and jeans. He'd let his hair and beard grow out in prison. He gave Jessica a lopsided smile as she approached.

"You've surrounded yourself with art." Jack's eyes sparkled. "We have art so we don't die of truth."

She responded with another Nietzsche quote: "Art is the proper task of life." Quoting philosophers was a game they played.

He laughed and moved in for a hug. "My heart is more yours now than it was two years ago when you kissed me and sent me to prison," he whispered in her ear.

A shiver ran down her spine. She whispered back, "Love is blind. Friendship just closes its eyes."

Jack pulled back from the embrace. "That's not what Nietzsche actually said."

"Are you two arguing philosophy already?" Holding a champagne flute, Lolita sidled up next to them. "Why don't you just get a room?"

Jessica felt her face get hot. She knew she must be beet red.

"Philosophy is a spectator sport," Jack said, raising

one eyebrow. "We only enjoy it when others are watching."

"You mean we're exhibitionists." Jessica laughed.

"The lack of privacy in prison forces exhibitionism." Behind his smile, she saw sorrow.

"I'm sorry." She put her hand on his sleeve.

"Don't be." He took her hand and kissed it. "It wasn't your fault. I'd do anything for you; you know that."

She blushed again.

"I agree with Lolita," Amber said. "You two should get a room."

"Don't you enjoy our company?" He asked with a playful grin.

"You know I love you both." Amber bounced up and down on her toes.

Jack stopped a passing waitress and handed champagne glasses all around. "I was sorry to hear about Gary."

Amber nodded and wrapped a lock of snaky hair around her finger.

"To absent friends." Jack raised his glass. "He was a good man."

He was a murderer. Jessica blew at her bangs and kept her mouth shut. She still felt bad about telling Detective Cormier her theory about the frog juice and the envelopes. She'd broken her promise to Amber. *But it was the right thing to do.* Intentionally or not, he'd poisoned three people with those envelopes. She thought of Nick. If only she'd stopped him from going to Chrissy's room . . .

"You look a million miles away, my Montana friend." Lolita put her arm around her. "Nick would have been proud of what you've done here."

"To absent friends." Jessica raised her glass. "We love life, not because we're used to living . . ."

Across the room, Bobby Charis caught her eye and raised his glass, too. He looked and smelled like Nick, but he didn't dress like him. *Nick wouldn't be caught dead in a pink tux.* Bobby had approved Mr. Schilling's pledge to the Center and the donation to help refugees. She hoped someday she'd get a chance to thank him in person.

Jessica clinked glasses with each of her friends. " . . . but because we're used to loving." She closed her eyes and thought of Nick.

ABOUT THE AUTHOR

Kelly Oliver is the award-winning and Amazon Best-selling author of *The Jessica James Mystery Series*, including **WOLF, COYOTE, FOX, JACKAL and VIPER. WOLF** won the *Independent Publisher's Gold Medal* for best Thriller/Mystery, was a finalist for the Foreward Magazine award for best mystery, and was voted number one in Women's Mysteries on Goodreads. **COYOTE** won a *Silver Falchion Award* for Best Mystery. **FOX** was a finalist for both the *Claymore* and the *Silver Falchion Awards*. JACKAL was a finalist for the *Mystery and Mayhem Award* and for the Silver Falchion Award.

She is the author of the middle grade mystery series, **The Pet Detective Mysteries. Kassy O'Roarke, Cub Reporter**, the first in the series is out now.

When she's not writing novels, Kelly is a Distinguished Professor of Philosophy at Vanderbilt University, and the author of fifteen nonfiction books, and over 100 articles, on issues such as the refugee crisis, campus rape, women and the media, animals and the environment. Her latest nonfiction book, **Hunting Girls: Sexual Violence from The Hunger Games to Campus**

Rape won a Choice Magazine Award for Outstanding title. She has published in *The New York Times* and *The Los Angeles Review of Books*, and has been featured on ABC news, CSPAN books, the Canadian Broadcasting Network, and various radio programs. To learn more about Kelly and her books, go to www.kellyoliverbooks.com.

If you liked this book, check out the others in the Jessica James Mystery series. And please leave a review on Amazon or Goodreads. Those reviews mean a lot to indie authors like me!! Thanks.

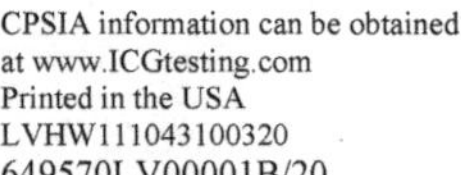
CPSIA information can be obtained
at www.ICGtesting.com
Printed in the USA
LVHW111043100320
649570LV00001B/20

9 780997 583687